LEADING

E-Learning

Here Is How You Can

- Chart Your Course

- Champion Implementation

- Ensure Success

ASTD
Linking People,
Learning & Performance

William Horton

Ordering information: Books published by ASTD can be ordered by calling 800.628.2783 or 703.683.8100, or via the Website at www.astd.org.

Library of Congress Catalog Card Number: 2001117679

ISBN: 1-56286-298-7

The following figures are printed with permission of William Horton Consulting: 1-2, 1-3, 2-3, 4-1, 6-1, 6-2, 6-3, 6-4, 6-5, 6-7, 6-8, 6-9, 7-1, 7-2, 7-3, 8-1, 8-2, 8-3, 8-4, 8-5, 8-6, 9-1, 9-2, 9-3, 10-1, 11-1, 12-1, 13-1, 13-2, 13-3.

Contents

Preface...vii

1. Welcome to the E-Learning Age **1**
    What Is E-Learning?...1
    How Has the Electronic Age Changed the Way
        People View Learning?...1
    How Is E-Learning Different From Traditional Training? 3
    A Short History of E-Learning 4
    What Is NOT E-Learning? 5
    What Is the Role of Teachers in E-Learning? 5
    Your Turn 6

2. Is the Time Right for E-Learning? **9**
    Is the Web Ready? 9
    Are Learners' Computers Ready?..10
    Are Learners Ready?...11
    Are Organizations Deploying E-Learning? 13
    Is Anybody Taking E-Learning? 14
    Your Turn 14

3. Why Consider E-Learning?..**17**
    Can E-Learning Teach as Effectively as Classroom Training Does? 17
    Does E-Learning Save Money?..19
    Can You Make Money With E-Learning?.................................24
    Your Turn 27

4. Where Should I Target E-Learning? **31**
    Why Not Just Replace Classroom Training?............................31
    What Are the Easy Targets?..32
    Pick Your Goals 33
    What Should You Consider When Deciding? 33
    Your Turn 38

5. How Can You Sell E-Learning? **41**

To Whom Must You Sell E-Learning?......................................41

How Can You Convince Them? 42

Speak the Language of Business 44

Sell Reality to Replace Hype...45

Our Turn: Selling Results, Not Illusions..................................46

Your Turn 47

6. What Kinds of E-Learning Can You Create? **49**

Self-Directed Web-Based Training 50

Facilitated Web-Based Training 51

Web-Conducted Classroom Course 52

Email Correspondence Course 53

Discussion Group Seminars...54

Guided Tours and Onscreen Workbooks 55

Learning Games 56

Telementoring and E-Coaching 57

Job Aids..58

Your Turn 59

7. Can You Blend E-Learning With Conventional Learning? **61**

Offer Proven Classroom Materials 61

Serve Sandwiches 62

Use Web Content in Classroom Training 63

Our Turn: A Case Study of Blended E-Learning 65

Your Turn 66

8. How Can You Develop E-Learning?...**69**

How Can You Start Off the Right Way?....................................69

How Is Developing E-Learning Different? 71

Standards 75

Your Turn 79

9. What Tools and Technology Will You Need? **83**

Computer Hardware for E-Learning..84

Network Connections for E-Learning..85

Software for E-Learning..87

How Do You Pick the Tools? 93

Your Turn 94

10. Whom Should You Have on Your E-Learning Team?.................................**97**

Assemble A Multitalented Team..97

Example of an E-Learning Team..104

Your Turn 108

11. Where Can You Find Help? **111**

How Much Do You Want to Do Yourself? 111

Who Can Help? 112

How Do You Screen Suppliers? 119

Your Turn 119

12. How Do You Launch Your Effort? **121**

Overview of a Plan 121

Your Turn 126

13. How Do You Deploy E-Learning Strategically? **129**

How Does E-Learning Promote a New Model for Training? 129

How Does E-Learning Support Knowledge Management? 130

How Does E-Learning Contribute to the Knowledge Economy? 131

What Is the Future of E-Learning? 133

Your Turn 134

14. Where Can You Learn More? **137**

What Organizations Should You Join? 137

What Books Should You Read? 138

Which Websites Should You Visit? 139

Periodicals, Paper, and Online 139

Where Can You Ask Questions? 140

What Conferences Should You Attend? 140

Your Turn 141

References 143

About the Author 147

Preface

I began writing this book 30 years ago. While still an undergraduate, I took a job at the Massachusetts Institute of Technology's Center for Advanced Engineering study, teaching a course in using computers to simulate social systems. The course required students, mostly midcareer engineers and government officials, to conduct simulations on teletype terminals connected to MIT's timesharing system. When I signed the contract, I did not realize that the course did not exist yet and that I would have to develop it. The only way I could stay ahead of the students was to put all course materials on the computer and let students print them out as they needed them.

As the course went on, students came to rely less and less on me as an instructor. Our lecture segments transformed into active discussions. Students became engaged in the exercises, trying variations and experiments on their own. And, my course design evolved to find new ways to challenge and enlighten students. In even this crude prototype of what we would today call blended e-learning, benefits were obvious if only to the tiny fraction of people with access to the necessary technology.

It has taken a long time, but finally many organizations have access to the powerful computers and networks that enable e-learning to take place. Today, as an e-learning consultant, I serve as an organizational midwife, helping deliver healthy e-learning programs. This book represents the best practices of hundreds of organizations that have moved into the e-learning age.

WHO IS THIS BOOK FOR?

This book is for people who want to lead their organization into the e-learning age. It is for those who want to see their organization use e-learning effectively and wisely, not just "do e-learning." It is for those who are willing to honestly deal with the complexities of e-learning to achieve its considerable potential. Moreover, it is for those who do not want suppliers and external consultants to take charge of the change, instead they want to lead their organizations into the realm of e-learning. These people are

- training managers
- team leaders of e-learning initiatives
- people who want to be a training manager or a team leader
- HR executives in charge of performance improvement or knowledge management
- trainers who want to launch new careers
- anyone who wants to contribute actively to this fundamental shift in the way training is performed.

WHAT WILL THIS BOOK DO FOR YOU?

Your organization may be a training department within a large corporation, a stand-alone training firm, or a group that wants to use e-learning to expand your current offerings. Whatever your title and whatever your group, this book can guide you in creating your strategy and tactics to move your organization into e-learning.

By reading this book, thinking about the issues it raises, completing the included activities, and consulting the companion Website, you will develop an e-learning strategy that fits the needs of your organization. You will assemble a plan to mastermind this momentous change—with the help of others. This book will provide you with a broad perspective of how e-learning fits into other corporate activities. It exposes you to the rich breadth of e-learning, the many forms it can take, and the tasks necessary to bring it about. This book previews other books in the e-learning arena and supplies you with a vocabulary of concepts and terms so you can deal with specialists and suppliers as an equal. It spells out a practical, common-sense, needs-based approach to corporate change.

WHAT'S SPECIAL ABOUT THIS BOOK?

This book is organized to make your learning experience as effective as possible. It is designed for quick skimming. Chapters and headings are organized around questions commonly asked by those making the transition to e-learning. This book is very action oriented. At the end of each chapter, "Your Turn" sections guide you in applying what you have just read to your organization's e-learning plan.

The book's companion Website (http://www.horton.com/leading) contains design forms, spreadsheets, live examples, and other resources to speed you on your way to e-learning.

This book draws on the experiences of hundreds of pioneers who developed the technology, instructional design, and business models that make e-learning a reality. Additionally, it draws on those brave souls who shared details of their failures, too. In writing this book, I was less of an author and more of a cartographer, crafting a map, not just from my own experiences, but from reports of explorers who have ranged the landscape. Use this map to chose your path and guide your explorations.

William Horton
August 2001

1

Welcome to the E-Learning Age

Web and Internet technologies are transforming our world, presenting opportunities we could only imagine a few years ago. Nowhere are these opportunities greater than in training and education. Every training department worldwide feels the winds of change at its back.

This book will help you start your organization on the road to e-learning. It is for managers, instructors, and instructional designers who want to move their organization into the e-learning age in an instructionally and financially responsible way. It is for those who can envision the benefits of new technologies while remaining objective about their limitations. This book is organized to help you answer the critical questions and make the crucial decisions necessary to integrate e-learning into your training efforts.

What Is E-Learning?

The first question to ask is "What is e-learning?" Many complex definitions of e-learning are circulating in the training arena, but this book relies upon this simple one: *E-learning is the use of Internet and digital technologies to create experiences that educate our fellow human beings.*

This definition is deliberately open-ended, allowing complete freedom as to how these experiences are formulated, organized, created, packaged, and marketed. As you will see later, that freedom is necessary to take full advantage of what e-learning offers.

How Has the Electronic Age Changed the Way People View Learning?

The traditional view of education as practiced in the classrooms of corporations, universities, and public schools is well established, highly refined, and largely unchanged for many years. In fact, it has often been remarked that a teacher from medieval times would feel right at home in the modern classroom, because so much learning still takes place under the direction of an instructor standing at the front of the classroom. The instructor determines the content, sequence, and pace of the course. The instructor keeps order and instills motivation. In addition, the instructor presents content, examines learners, and supplies feedback. In many ways, the instructor *is* the course (figure 1-1).

As in medieval times, much education and training today is "just-in-case" learning. Students learn facts and skills just in case they may need them sometime in the future. Courses tend to be comprehensive, teaching all about the subject—everything any student may need to know.

For learners in the traditional model, learning is a full-time activity. It is the profession of students. Even full-time corporate staff are expected to give their full attention to learning while they are in the classroom. Often classrooms are specifically located so that learners are isolated from their work duties.

Change is happening rapidly in the training classroom. Not only does training look different during the e-age because we are using new technologies to deliver training in the classroom and on the job, but we also hold a *completely new view of what we mean by learning and how it takes place.*

The e-age view of learning is quite different. Learning can take place anywhere it is needed, typically within the work environment at the time where the need for learning manifests itself. Learning is not a separate cloistered event but a regular part of everyday life (figure 1-2).

Learners choose when to seek learning and what specific knowledge or skills they will acquire, and it is the learner who decides when to quit. This just-in-time, just-enough philosophy tends to deliver learning in small units spread over a longer period of time. The e-age view is one of continual, life-

Figure 1-1. "The Country School" by Winslow Homer, 1871, St. Louis Museum of Art.

Source: Electronic image from ArtsEdsNet. J. Paul Getty Trust. (1999).
http://www.artsednet.getty.edu/ArtsEdNet/Images/P/school.html.

Figure 1-2. E-learning can happen anytime, anywhere.

long learning controlled by the learner. Such a view is not new, but until now we have lacked the technologies to make it practical.

HOW IS E-LEARNING DIFFERENT FROM TRADITIONAL TRAINING?

E-technologies do not change how human beings learn. What technology does is to remove constraints on the kinds of learning experiences we can economically and practically create.

In e-learning, it is the learner, not the instructor, who controls the pace and order of learning experiences—and, to some extent, the very selection of which learning experiences are a part of the course. Each learner may experience a different course through the same collection of materials.

E-learning can occur when and where each learner wants it to, making it easier to integrate learning with daily work. But, in e-learning, learners are never more than a mouse click from quitting. They can drop out at any moment. Designers can never take the motivation of the learner for granted.

In e-learning, because learners are not physically present, it is hard to know their private concerns, thoughts, and feelings. We cannot observe body language or facial expressions. Nor can we always listen to the tone of voice or watch gestures as learners ask questions or make comments. E-learning can be lonely learning. The camaraderie of the classroom is hard to re-create over global networks.

The differences between classroom learning and e-learning rewrite the rules of learning. Designs and deployments of e-learning that accommodate these and other differences between traditional and e-learning environments have greater chances of success.

A SHORT HISTORY OF E-LEARNING

Although the term *e-learning* is new, the concept of using technology and communication infrastructure to enable new forms of learning is well established. E-learning has its roots in postal correspondence courses, starting with Sir Isaac Pitman's 1840 course in shorthand. Such courses constituted the first attempt to use communication infrastructure to extend training beyond the sound of the human voice.

> ### Still Teaching After All These Years
>
> In 1840 Sir Isaac Pitman began using the Penny Post to teach his phonetic shorthand system across England. Today the company he founded is still teaching. Pitman Training (www.pitman-training.com) offers a range of classroom and self-study vocational courses throughout the United Kingdom and Ireland.

Postal correspondence courses proved many of the concepts at the core of e-learning: that students could pace their own learning, that learning was possible without face-to-face contact, that large numbers of students could be taught independently on separate schedules. In fact, it should come as no surprise, then, that one of the earliest forms of successful e-learning was the email correspondence course. (Such courses are described in chapter 6.)

The first use of computers in teaching was the collaboration between Stanford University and IBM in the late 1950s. Although the effectiveness of using mainframe computers to administer drill-and-practice exercises to elementary school children proved questionable, the potential was clearly visible. From such crude experiments grew the PLATO system, with its more sophisticated evaluation and branching, which was used to deliver over 40 million hours of instruction on a variety of sophisticated subjects from the mid-1960s through the mid-1980s.

The arrival of the PC eliminated the requirement for an expensive mainframe computer and accompanying terminals. It also added the possibility of advanced graphics, animation, voice, and other media. The development of CD-ROM storage simplified the task of housing and distributing substantial courses.

The development of the World Wide Web in the 1990s added new technologies, which further removed barriers to effective distance learning by computer. Hypertext markup language (HTML) provided an easy, standardized way to construct computer displays, and the Internet supplied the means of distributing training broadly from a central, easily updated source. Email, newsgroups, and other collaboration media all showed that e-learning need not be the lonely, slow-paced effort of postal correspondence courses 160 years earlier.

WHAT IS NOT E-LEARNING?

There is considerable disagreement about the nature of e-learning and where that term should be applied. Proponents and opponents of e-learning seem to use the term to suit their positions. Suppliers slap it on products with illogical abandon. For example, here is a list of a few things that e-learning is not:

- *It's not just Web-casting lectures.* Today, just about anybody can point a videocamera at someone and transmit the resulting images over the Internet to remote viewers. Watching small, jerky, grainy images of a poorly lit, awkward, self-conscious lecturer effects very little learning, however. Regardless of whether the video streams, screams, or beams, a video talking head is seldom effective training without an accompaniment of engaging activities and meaningful feedback.
- *It's not training materials dumped online.* Converting training manuals or slide presentations to HTML or some other Web-viewable format creates another form of pseudo-e-learning. Such conversions cannot stand alone and seldom succeed. Both IBM and Air Canada found they could not simply and inexpensively convert classroom courses and documents to e-learning (Hall, 2000b), but providing classroom materials is not a bad idea. (For some suggestions on how to use existing materials, see chapter 7.)
- *It's not limited to formal courses.* Most training professionals think of units of learning as packaged courses, that is, well-defined, substantive bodies of instruction conducted as a scheduled sequence of events. E-learning may certainly provide courses, but it also embraces other forms of learning, such as electronic job aids, simulations, learning games, glossaries, virtual museums, telementoring, and guided tours. (You can link to examples of some of these forms from this book's companion Website at www.horton.com/leading/.) An e-learning solution is not necessarily a course as you may be accustomed to thinking about it.
- *It's not computers teaching people.* Frequently those opposed to or frightened by e-learning charge that computers cannot teach people; ergo, e-learning cannot work. Although computers and networks are a part of e-learning, they are the medium, not the genesis, of learning. Computers and networks are just the medium whereby teachers can trigger learning experiences in learners, like the chalkboard in a classroom.

WHAT IS THE ROLE OF TEACHERS IN E-LEARNING?

If e-learning has no fixed classrooms, then what will become of classroom teachers? Well, e-learning does not eliminate teachers, but it does fundamentally redefine their roles. In the classroom, it is the instructor who teaches; in e-learning, it is the designer who teaches.

Compare the roles of classroom instructors and e-learning designers (figure 1-3). How do instructors teach in the classroom? They lecture, demonstrate skills, tell stories, ask questions, answer questions, assign tasks, critique work, conduct tests, and assign grades. What do e-learning designers do? They select material, write text, draw pictures, shoot video, create animation, program interactivity, and configure technology. The activities of these two kinds of teachers may seem completely different until we ask "Why?" In both cases, their goal is to provoke learning experiences.

In the classroom, teachers trigger learning experiences in the minds of students, but it is the students themselves who do the learning. Teachers simply provide the environment and resources necessary for learning to take place. In e-learning, there is no instructor; but, there is a designer who triggers the same learning experiences. This designer, perhaps aided by a facilitator, must do all the things done by a classroom instructor—but by remote control.

Figure 1-3. Comparing the roles of classroom instructors and e-learning designers.

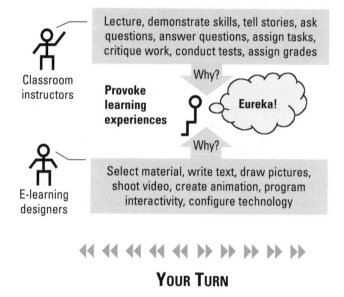

YOUR TURN

Each chapter ends with some activities to help you take the first steps in moving your organization to e-learning. No heavy lifting is required. These activities can be done from your computer or reading chair. They just involve thinking deeply about how the ideas in the chapter apply to your organization.

If you do not want to write in this book, just go to the book's companion Website (www.horton.com/leading/) where you can download and print blank copies of these activities. Regardless of whether you write your answers in this book, on the blank forms you print, or in a notebook, remember to refer to them often as you plan your first e-learning projects.

Why are you reading this book? Did your boss assign you e-learning as a responsibility? Are you looking for a career change? Take a minute or two to assess your personal goals for involvement in e-learning using worksheet 1-1.

Worksheet 1-1. Identifying your goals in the realm of e-learning.		
Your Personal Goal for Involvement in E-Learning	**Date for Accomplishing This Goal**	**Done? (✔)**

If you have not already, take at least three sample e-learning courses. To find some free samples, search the Web for "e-learning example" or similar phrases. Try to find three quite different forms of e-learning. After you complete the sample courses, use worksheet 1-2 to answer some questions about each course.

Worksheet 1-2. Evaluate your e-learning experience.		
Course	**How Was the E-Learning Different From Classroom Training?**	**How Was the E-Learning Different From What You Expected?**

Catalog the uses of e-learning in your organization (worksheet 1-3). If you can't find any, determine if any employees have taken professional development courses on their own. Check with the information technology department to see if any technicians have used e-learning to upgrade their technical skills. Remember, e-learning is not just formal courses. It can include any use of Internet and Web technologies to increase knowledge, improve skills, or change attitudes.

Worksheet 1-3. Evaluate the use of e-learning in your organization.

Group	What E-Learning Courses Have Been Taken?	For What Purpose?

2

Is the Time Right for E-Learning?

Is e-learning ready for use by mainstream training organizations or only by a technological and economic elite? Do enough organizations and individuals possess the required budgets, technologies, and skills? Are learners ready to move out of a classroom setting to acquire the skills and knowledge they need? You must answer these questions before committing even a part of your organization to the e-learning path.

IS THE WEB READY?

The World Wide Web is real. It is here now. It is changing our lives in ways blatant and subtle. And the Web keeps growing and growing—not just in width and height but in depth as well. It is this growth that enables the e-learning revolution. How big is the Web? Here are some recent (and already outdated) statistics that you may find interesting:

- 407 million people use the Web worldwide, 167 million of those in the United States and Canada (Nua Inc., 2000a).
- 9.6 million Websites and 98 million Internet hosts (Telcordia Technologies, 2000) deliver over a billion page-views each day (Mack, 1999).
- 156 million U.S. residents (56 percent of the population) have Internet access from home, and 40 million have access from work (Nua Inc., 2000b). By 2004, 90 percent of U.S. households should have Internet access (Strategis Group, 2000).
- In the United States and Canada in 1999, more than 40 percent of the population used the Web regularly, and 92 million users were older than 16 years (Lieb, 2000).

■ 84 percent of U.S. college students have Web access (internet.com Corp., 1999). In 1999, 95 percent of U.S. public schools had Internet access, and 89 percent of those had ISDN or higher speed connections (Riley, Holleman, and Roberts, 2000).

■ The number of Web users doubled in the 15 months ending December 2000 (Nua Inc., 2000c). In July 2000, the number of Internet hosts was growing at 65 percent per year (Internet Software Consortium, 2000).

Access to the Web varies around the globe. As shown in figure 2-1, the United States, Canada, and western Europe are well connected to the Internet, though some other countries, especially developing countries, are just getting wired.

But don't jump to conclusions: Averages are not particulars. Although the percentage of the population connected to the Web may be low in a specific country, the percentage of your potential learners may be high, especially if they work in high-technology industries or for international companies.

ARE LEARNERS' COMPUTERS READY?

Compared to the PCs of five years ago, today's models run eight times faster, have eight times more memory, sport disks 32 times larger, communicate three times faster, and cost 40 percent less. This rate of progress seems set to continue. As a

Figure 2-1. Who has access to the Web?

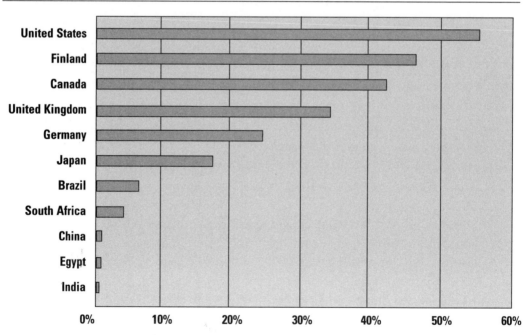

Source: Nua Inc. (2000c) and United Nations (2001).

result, electronic training solutions that were impossible a few years ago are mainstream today. Ones that we can only imagine today will be practical soon.

One critical area of technological advancement is in the speed of communication. As shown in figure 2-2, most Americans have at least moderate speed access. However, the ability to use video and rich multimedia in e-learning hinges on the availability of high-speed (broadband) network connections. In the United States, access to high-speed access through digital subscriber line (DSL), cable modem, or other broadband service is growing at a rate of about 230 percent per year, and, by 2005, the majority of Americans should have high-speed access from home (internet.com Corp., 2001).

The technology required for e-learning is not extreme. Course authors who rely on sound instructional design, intriguing interactivity, and low-bandwidth graphics and animations instead of video talking heads and twirling, three-dimensional logos are discovering that even older PCs with modem connections can deliver highly effective e-learning. Chapter 9 will help you decide exactly what technology you and your learners require.

ARE LEARNERS READY?

The common stereotype of an Internet user is a young, white, male techno-geek, typically an information technology professional within a technical organization. Recent statistics show that stereotype is wrong:

- Over half of U.S. Web users are women (Rickert and Sacharow, 2000).
- The fastest growing age segment of Web users is those over age 55 (internet.com Corp., 2000).

Figure 2-2. U.S. Internet connection speeds, December 2000.

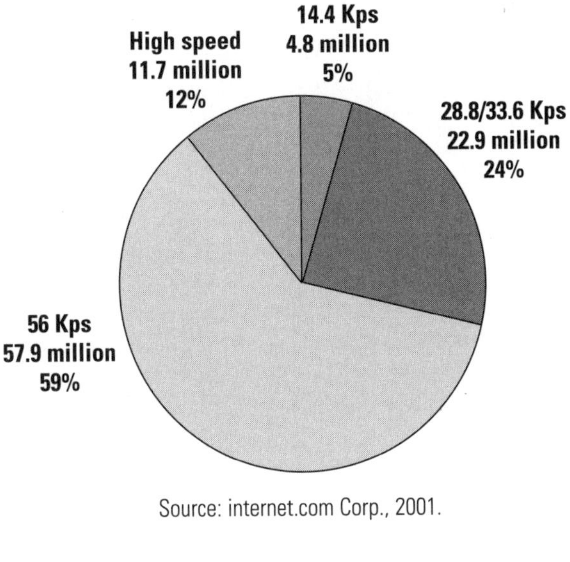

Source: internet.com Corp., 2001.

■ According to a 2000 Forrester Research (www.forrester.com) report, 40 percent of blacks and 43 percent of Hispanics used the Internet, and the number of blacks and Hispanics with Internet access from home doubled between February 1999 and October 2000 (National Telecommunications and Information Administration, 2000).

■ Internet usage by low-income Americans (less than $25,000 per year household income) increased 50 percent in 2000, more than twice the rate of increase for Internet usage as a whole (Rickert, 2000). By 1999, 31 percent of households with incomes below $20,000 per year had computers (Riley, Holleman, and Roberts, 2000).

■ The first phase of a two-phase study found that 80 percent of physicians across 11 North American, European, and Asian countries own a computer and that 44 percent of these physicians have accessed the Internet (WebSurveyResearch, 2000). Most of the physicians surveyed use the Internet for informational or educational purposes, including gathering

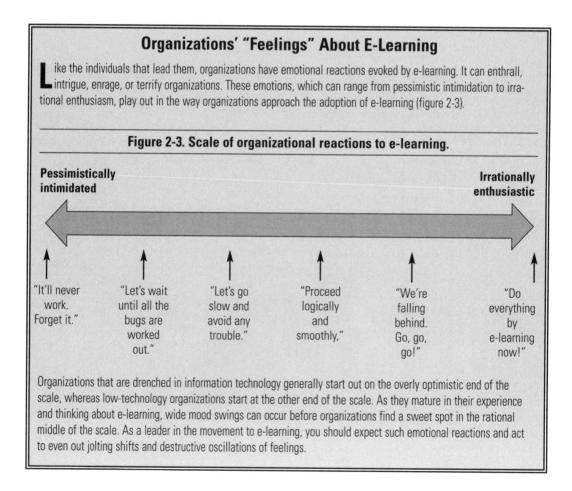

Organizations' "Feelings" About E-Learning

Like the individuals that lead them, organizations have emotional reactions evoked by e-learning. It can enthrall, intrigue, enrage, or terrify organizations. These emotions, which can range from pessimistic intimidation to irrational enthusiasm, play out in the way organizations approach the adoption of e-learning (figure 2-3).

Figure 2-3. Scale of organizational reactions to e-learning.

Pessimistically intimidated ← → **Irrationally enthusiastic**

"It'll never work. Forget it."

"Let's wait until all the bugs are worked out."

"Let's go slow and avoid any trouble."

"Proceed logically and smoothly,"

"We're falling behind. Go, go, go!"

"Do everything by e-learning now!"

Organizations that are drenched in information technology generally start out on the overly optimistic end of the scale, whereas low-technology organizations start at the other end of the scale. As they mature in their experience and thinking about e-learning, wide mood swings can occur before organizations find a sweet spot in the rational middle of the scale. As a leader in the movement to e-learning, you should expect such emotional reactions and act to even out jolting shifts and destructive oscillations of feelings.

information about drugs or medical products (75 percent) or treatments (68 percent), and taking continuing medical education courses (45 percent).

■ Recently, Ford, American Airlines, and Delta Airlines announced programs to equip each of their employees with a PC with an Internet connection.

Clearly, the so-called digital divide separating the technological elite from the masses is closing to a bridgeable ravine. The upshot of this growing acceptance of the Web is that e-learning can reach many different types of people in many different venues. Many of those who need e-learning are already accustomed to looking for what they need from the Internet. Not only are learners ready for e-learning, they are *demanding* the kinds of training that e-learning can deliver. A Gallup Organization survey of U.S. workers found that they strongly preferred informal, self-paced, on-the-job training to formal classroom training (Schaaf, 1998).

ARE ORGANIZATIONS DEPLOYING E-LEARNING?

The Web is real and so is e-learning. E-learning is attracting attention, technology, and money. Corporations and universities are not hesitating to use e-learning. In 1999, 41 percent of large organizations offered some form of e-learning, and 92 percent said they planned to do so within the year (Barron and Rickelman, 1999). That same year, nearly half of all colleges and universities provided some form of online education (Kestenbaum, 1998), and that number is expected to double by 2004 (IDC, 2000). In a 2000 survey, Drake Beam Morin, a global employment consulting firm, found that 54 percent of firms were using e-learning to teach technical skills and 47 percent to teach professional skills (Smith, 2000).

U-Turn or Just a Bend in the Road?

The 2001 ASTD State of the Industry Report (ASTD, 2001) reported that the amount of training delivered by e-learning, as described by its benchmarking service participants, actually peaked at 9.1 percent in 1997 and declined to 8.5 percent in 1998 and 8.4 percent in 1999. Likewise, two-year-out projections for future use of e-learning declined from the 1998 estimate that by 2000, 23 percent of all training would be done by e-learning to the 2000 estimate of 18.2 percent by 2002.

Some have cited these figures as evidence that the e-learning "fad" is fizzling out. Others see it as a pause to catch up. The report cited the need to correct early negative experiences with immature e-learning offerings and the time required to upgrade internal infrastructure to handle e-learning. Some organizations are finding that they cannot just dump their classroom materials onto the Web and expect effective learning to take place.

Still, organizations remained optimistic about e-learning, projecting the use of learning technologies to rise from 14.9 percent of all training in 1999 to 24.4 percent in 2002. All categories of survey participants said, that by 2002, intranets would be the most widely used learning technology, replacing CD-ROMs at the top of the list.

Neither the ASTD report nor any of the other market studies cited elsewhere in this chapter projected that e-learning would fade away. Though different authorities disagree on the rate of growth, all concur that e-learning will mature to become a major force in training.

IS ANYBODY TAKING E-LEARNING?

Not only are organizations offering e-learning, learners are snapping it up. E-learning has moved from the educational fringe toward the mainstream in terms of public and corporate acceptance and appreciation.

Use of e-learning in preparing for information technology certification exams rose threefold in 1999 (Clark and Johnson, 1999). At Cisco, where 80 percent of sales and technical training is available electronically, 80 percent of the sales staff use e-learning (Hall, 2000b). Throughout Cisco, 13,000 employees registered for e-learning within a year. At Boeing, over 40,000 employees have taken internal e-learning courses (Porter, 1999).

But, e-learning is not just for the technical training niche. A study by Drake Beam Morin found that 94 percent of training and HR professionals believe that e-learning is effective for teaching professional development. Furthermore, 74 percent expect it to become the mainstream (Smith, 2000).

It has never been so easy to learn so much about so many different topics, thanks to e-learning. And, the public is becoming aware of that fact. In 1999, Cisco Systems spent over $20 million for television advertisements featuring e-learning (Hall, 2000a). Acceptance of computer-based learning is clearly growing: 69 percent of Americans believe that using computer technology has improved the quality of instructions at their local schools, and 82 percent believe that schools should invest in additional computer technology (Riley, Holleman, and Roberts, 2000).

The University of Phoenix Online now offers complete degree programs over the Internet (University of Phoenix, 2000). Many other universities and community colleges offer myriad courses in online formats, and many professors rely upon e-learning to some extent. A quick search on the Internet reveals hundreds, if not thousands, of educational organizations offering a spectrum of online courses that ranges from U.S. politics and sports medicine to psychology of death and silversmithing.

YOUR TURN

Yeah, yeah, lots of people are using e-learning, but your situation is unique. Your organization may not fit the trend or want to. Take a few minutes to assess your organization's readiness for e-learning by using worksheet 2-1.

How does your organization feel about e-learning? Where along the scale of e-learning would you rate your organization (figure 2-3)? Use worksheet 2-2 to find out.

	Worksheet 2-1. Is your organization ready for e-learning?		
#	**Questions About Your Organization**	**Yes (✔)**	**No (✔)**
1	Do learners have access to computers capable of displaying e-learning materials?		
2	Does the organization have network and Internet connections fast enough to support e-learning?		
3	Is technical support available to help e-learners over hurdles?		
4	Do potential e-learners possess the necessary computer skills?		
5	Are instructors and instructional designers knowledgeable about e-learning?		
6	Does top management support e-learning?		
7	Do the management teams for training, information technology, and HR understand and support e-learning?		

For each question with a "no" response . . .

#	**What steps will you take to change the answer to "Yes"?**

Worksheet 2-2. Where is my organization on the scale of reactions to e-learning?

My organization is at _____.

It should be at _____.

What can I do to get it from where it is to where it should be along this scale?

1. _____.

2. _____.

3. _____.

4. _____.

5. _____.

3

Why Consider E-Learning?

E-learning is an interesting social and technological phenomenon. But does it really work for organizations? Can it teach as effectively as classroom training? Can it save money? Can it make money? The answers to these questions build a compelling case for trying e-learning.

CAN E-LEARNING TEACH AS EFFECTIVELY AS CLASSROOM TRAINING DOES?

Many organizations are discovering that e-learning can be as effective as classroom training at a fraction of the cost. Perhaps you have heard of the no-significant-difference phenomenon. Several researchers have documented the lack of a statistically significant difference among the effectiveness of various training technologies. For example, education researcher Thomas Russell (1999) has listed 355 research reports and other studies that found no meaningful difference in grades, satisfaction, or effectiveness among training conducted in classrooms, by postal correspondence, with videotapes, or through e-learning. If there is no significant difference among the potential effectiveness of various alternatives, then training providers can choose the most economical and practical alternative—which, in many cases, will be e-learning.

Even Immature E-Learning Works

Most studies that compared e-learning to other technologies tended to understate the potential of e-learning. Often these studies compared an established and perfected form of training to initial efforts in an immature form. Many of the e-learning courses that were not significantly different from classroom training in terms of effectiveness were the first efforts by designers. Many of the courses were taught by facilitators who had no experience teaching via the Web. Often the e-learning course was the first one taken by students and marked the first time they had used several new technologies such as chat sessions, discussion groups, screen-sharing sessions, or videoconferencing. Considering all these limitations, we can only expect that future e-learning efforts will score even better against traditional training technologies and methods.

E-Learning Can Teach Faster

Not all studies showed no significant difference between e-learning and other methods. Several studies found that e-learning could teach the same material in less time. Consider these examples:

- ASK International (1999) reduced one-week training courses to equally effective six-hour courses, yielding an 80 percent reduction in cost.
- Learners in an online course by the Mortgage Bankers Association of America covered the same material in less time but in greater depth than their classroom counterparts (Monahan, 1998).
- Bank & Trust of Litchfield, Illinois, cut in half the time required to train new tellers (Karon, 2000).
- Intel, by embedding e-learning into applications, reduced the maximum time off the job for training technicians from 12 hours per technician to just two hours (Hall, 2000b).
- Cisco has cut the time to get new manufacturing workers up to full productivity from 12 weeks to four weeks (Hall, 2000b).
- Hewlett Packard reduced the time required to train a global sales force from one year to one month (Picard, 1996). In doing so they cut training costs by 78 percent.

As faster communications links allow greater use of multimedia, we can expect further time savings. A review of more than 40 studies of training projects in industry, military, and education found that multimedia reduced training time by an average of 31 percent (Fletcher, 1990). A survey of 30 studies by Bradley Associates (1994) found that multimedia training reduced training time by 50 percent. Six controlled studies at Federal Express, Xerox, IBM, and other companies found that multimedia training required 38 percent to 70 percent less time than classroom training (Adams, 1992).

E-Learning Can Teach Better

When properly designed, targeted, and deployed, e-learning can produce better results than classroom training. One e-learning course that did show a statistically significant improvement over classroom training was, appropriately enough, a course on statistics offered by Cal State Northridge. In this course, students scored 20 percent higher on the final exam than those who took the classroom version. Furthermore, the students who took the e-learning version felt more confident about math and said that they had better communications with fellow students (Schutte, 1997).

With e-learning at Office Depot, retention increased by 25 percent and satisfaction by 30 percent. Switching to e-learning doubled enrollment and cut costs by 80 percent (Maher, 1998).

A range of studies in public education found that "with technology student achievement increases, students can learn more in less time and undertake more ambitious school projects, and that students have more positive attitudes toward classes that use technology" (Riley, Holleman, and Roberts, 2000). Courses that incorporate meaningful interactivity and multimedia produce better results. A review of many different studies of multimedia learning programs in industry, the military, and education found a 15 percent to 25 percent improvement in learning (Fletcher, 1990). A review of six studies comparing multimedia learning to conventional classroom training found multimedia learning resulted in 56 percent greater learning, 50 percent to 60 percent better consistency, and 25 percent to 50 percent higher retention (Adams, 1992).

DOES E-LEARNING SAVE MONEY?

One of the greatest promises of e-learning is to reduce greatly the cost of training large numbers of learners. But what does experience with e-learning suggest about its economics? Here are some great examples of how companies are saving money with e-learning:

- MCI WorldCom cut training costs $5.6 million on one project (Kroll, 1999). Using e-learning, they trained 7,000 technicians at 800 different locations. On projects like these, they report a 237 percent return-on-investment (ROI) (Fryer, 1998).
- Aetna reduced the costs for training 3,000 employees by $3 million—a savings of $1,000 per employee. Aetna also cut the cost of traveling to training classes by $4,166 per person trained (Kroll, 1999).
- Buckman Laboratories cut the costs of training employees to use its e-mail system by 84 percent (Gillette, 1998).
- Cisco reduced training costs from $1,500 per person to just $120—a 92 percent reduction (Terry, 1998).
- Training for Novel certification was reduced from over $1,800 to around $800 per person (Terry, 1998).
- A 2.5-hour course developed by Bell Canada yielded a 288 percent ROI, paying back its development costs after only 111 learners; a 4-hour course yielded a 3,283 percent ROI, paying back its development costs after only four learners (Whalen and Wright, 2000).

- Storage Technology reduced training costs from \$3,291,327 to \$1,748,327 by switching from a conventional classroom course to e-learning (Hall, 2000a).
- Eli Lilly and Co. saved \$800,000 in travel and salary costs the first year of its e-learning training program (McGee, 1998).
- A 5-year study by PriceWaterhouseCoopers of its internal e-learning project found a cost per student of \$106, compared to \$760 per learner for conventional classroom training (Hall, 2000a).
- Sun Microsystems cut costs for sales training by \$3.5 million. More significantly, Sun was able to cut the time participants had to spend away from their jobs by 80 percent (Densford, 1998).

Awareness of the economy of e-learning is spreading. Training managers and learners interviewed by the Gartner Group in late 1999 rated the cost-effectiveness of e-learning as nine on a 10-point scale as compared to a 4 for classroom training (Anonymous, 2000).

To see how e-learning can save a training organization money, consider the case of the fictitious company Gizbotics International. Gizbotics is preparing to launch its new line of fourth-generation gizbots. To do so, it must train its global sales force of 200 sales representatives on the benefits, features, and robo-ethics of this new product line.

Ohle Schulle, chief executive officer of Gizbotics, recalling new product launches, is concerned about the cost of such a massive training program. Schulle asks Nina Newview, head of training for Gizbotics, to investigate whether this new e-learning stuff could help. Nina has heard of the potential of e-learning to save money but is concerned about the risks of adopting a new approach without careful analysis. So, she sets out to estimate the costs of providing the required training through traditional classroom methods and through e-learning.

A quick review of the records of the last product launch reveals the enormity of the task. The 200 sales representatives are scattered over the globe, and most will have to travel to the site of training. Because gizbots are highly technical products, training for a new product line may require 4 full days in the classroom.

Costs of Developing Courses

The first costs Nina must confront are the costs of developing the training course. From records on past training programs, she estimates a figure of \$10,000 per day of classroom training. These costs include preparing presentation graphics and handouts and training the trainers. For 4 days of training, she expects development to cost \$40,000.

For e-learning, Nina is a little less sure of development costs. She has heard that e-learning takes four times as much work to develop because everything must be written down, and complex ideas must be expressed in multimedia. To be safe, she doubles the estimate to account for the fact that much of the work on an e-learning project will require hiring technical specialists and consultants whose fees exceed the baseline salaries of the instructors who develop classroom training. Thus, Nina estimates that each day of e-learning will cost $80,000 to develop.

But how many days of e-learning will be required? Nina has heard of the learning compression that takes place with e-learning. Supposedly, people can learn the same amount of material in less time. She is tempted to reduce the number of days of e-learning from 4 to 3 to take this compression into account. Nevertheless, Nina realizes that this will be the first experience with e-learning for many of the salesforce, so she decides to assume 4 days of e-learning. She also makes a note to provide technical support to help the remote learners get started. So, for development costs, Nina's estimates are:

	Classroom	E-Learning
Cost per day of training	$10,000	$80,000
Number of days of training	4	4
Total development costs	$40,000	$320,000
(cost/day × number of days)		

"Yikes, this is not looking good," moans Nina. "Well, I won't panic until I see all the costs," she says to herself.

Costs of Conducting Training

Next, Nina decides to consider the costs of conducting the training. For classroom training, she will need to pay for classroom facilities as well as the salary of the instructor. She decides to base her estimate on a class size of 20 students. That means she must conduct 10 classes to train the 200 sales representatives. That works out to 40 class days to complete the classroom training.

For classroom facilities, Nina will need a classroom and a breakout room. Her department owns these facilities, but she must pay an amortized cost of $500 per day to use them. For the required 40 training days, classroom facilities will cost $20,000

From department budgets, she sees that each day of instructor time costs $800 including salary, benefits, office space, and administrative support. Therefore, 40 class days will cost $32,000 in instructor time.

Because Nina decides to base her estimate on self-directed e-learning, no facilitator or instructor is required. E-learning will require space on a Web server. Nina obtains a price of $10,000 for the purchase and setup of an in-house Web server. The anticipated training program will not exhaust the server's capabilities, so the server will be available for other uses as well. Knowing Gizbotic's concern about data security and wanting to be conservative in her estimates, Nina decides to use the full $10,000 cost in her estimate. Nina adds up the costs for offering the training:

	Classroom	E-Learning
Classroom facilities	$20,000	—
Instructor time	$32,000	—
Web server	—	$10,000
Total offering costs	$52,000	$10,000

Although e-learning has substantially lower offering costs, these savings come nowhere close to offsetting the higher development costs. To find savings, Nina must look further.

Costs Due to Learners

Next Nina considers the additional costs of providing training to each individual learner. Training sales representatives in the classroom requires pulling them out of the field. This results in two costs. First, sales representatives must travel to the site of training. Nina estimates that the average travel costs (including air fare, hotel, meals, and taxi fares) will average $2,000 per sales representative attending four days of classroom training. A second cost comes from the sales lost when sales representatives are not in the field. From the vice president of sales, Nina obtains a figure of $20,000 as the sales volume lost for each day that a sales representative is not in the field. From accounting, she learns that the profit margin on such sales is 20 percent. Therefore, the opportunity cost of the missing sales is 20 percent of $20,000, or $4,000, for each day that the sales representative is missing from the field.

How many days will the sales representative miss? Because they must travel to obtain the training, Nina estimates that on average each sales representative will miss one day for travel in addition to the four days of training. So, for classroom training, sales representatives will miss five days in the field, costing the company $20,000 for each sales representative being trained in the classroom.

How about for e-learning? Well, no travel days are required, so at first Nina plans to use the four-day training period as the time away from the field. Realizing that this is a critical assumption, she telephones a few sales representatives and asks their opinions of e-learning. She learns that most sales representatives have laptop computers, which they carry home. Furthermore, most say they would prefer to take some of the training during weekends and evenings so that they do not miss out on sales opportunities. An informal survey convinces Nina that sales representatives will take 25 percent of the e-learning at home, so they will miss just three days of sales. The profit lost while sales reps are taking e-learning will be $4,000 times three days, or $12,000, per sales representative.

Just as Nina is ready to wrap up her calculations, she comes across the note she wrote to remind herself to include the cost of providing technical support to the learners. Gizbotic's information technology (IT) department agrees to provide telephone support to sales representatives taking e-learning. The IT department will charge the training department $100 per hour of support provided. Nina, realizing that sales reps use their laptop computers routinely to enter orders and check out competitors' Websites, estimates that each sales representative may require two hours of telephone support.

Her tally for costs due to learners looks something like this:

	Classroom	E-Learning
Travel	$2,000	—
Lost profit on sales	$20,000	$12,000
Technical support	—	$200
Total cost per learner	$22,000	$12,200
Number of learners	200	200
Total costs due to learners	$4,400,000	$2,440,000
(cost/learner × number of learners)		

Nina blinks, rubs her eyes, and rechecks her figures. The savings in travel and time off the job really add up when multiplied by the number of potential learners.

Total Costs

Finally, Nina adds up the separate cost figures:

	Classroom	E-Learning
Costs of developing courses	$40,000	$320,000
Costs of conducting training	$52,000	$10,000
Costs due to learners	$4,400,000	$2,440,000
Total costs	$4,492,000	$2,770,000

Wow! E-learning offers a potential savings of $1,722,000, or 38 percent, over the cost of classroom training. *Caveat emptor:* The figures in the preceding example are reasonable but may bear no resemblance to the ones for your organization's situation. Use these calculations as a model for your own. If you want to play around with the figures, you can download a spreadsheet containing this example from the companion Website for this book at www.horton.com/leading.

CAN YOU MAKE MONEY WITH E-LEARNING?

Many organizations see e-learning as a business opportunity. They hope to develop and offer e-learning courses for profit. Many small- and medium-sized training and consulting firms hope to complement their offerings of classroom workshops and seminars with e-learning courses. But first, they want to know whether such moves will prove profitable.

As more and more corporate training departments are expected to serve as profit centers rather than "money sinks," the need to assess the business potential of e-learning has become a necessity. Some internal training departments have evolved to offer courses to customers and suppliers of their organizations as well as to their employees. Some face the prospect and opportunity of being spun off as a separate company altogether. For these training departments, developing a sound for-profit business model is not an academic exercise. Certainly e-learning has spawned its share of get-rich-quick schemes. To make sure your plan is realistic, take a few moments to consider the business market for e-learning.

How Big Is the E-Learning Market?

The market for e-learning is growing and is nowhere near saturation. A Merrill Lynch study entitled "The Book of Knowledge: Investing in the Growing Education and Training Industry" found that the market for education and training was vast. Merrill Lynch estimated that the market within corporations in the United States alone is $96 billion (Moe, 1999). The total market in the United States, including the private and public education sectors, is $740 billion. Worldwide, the market is $2 trillion.

E-learning is taking an increasing portion of that market. In 2000, expenditures for e-learning should exceed $2 billion and reach $11 billion by 2003 (Urdan and Weggen, 2000). Addressing the Comdex technology conference, John Chambers, president and chief executive officer of Cisco Systems, boldly stated the potential for e-learning: "Education over the Internet is going to be so big it is going to make e-mail usage look like a rounding error in terms of the Internet capacity it will consume."

The Business Model

If you are considering e-learning as a means to improve your department's bottom line, develop a financial model and do the math. Consider a fictional character named Kevin Kronor who used a simple, back-of-the-envelope model that touches on some of the main factors that influence e-learning for profit.

Kevin wants to develop and market courses over the Web. Kevin also wants to make a profit. First, he starts by calculating how much money he can take in by offering courses. Kevin then checks the market and decides that he can charge $50 per enrollment in each course and can attract 1,000 learners per year.

Enrollment fee per learner	$50
Number of learners per year	1,000
Total annual revenue	$50,000

His revenues, then, should be $50,000 per year for each course he offers. For each course, Kevin estimates development will cost $100,000. He expects to be able to offer each course for four years before replacing it. Dividing the development cost by the lifespan, he spreads the development cost over four years. Believing that interest rates and inflation will remain low over the next few years, Kevin decides not to adjust that figure. To the development cost, Kevin adds $15,000 per year to pay for hosting and maintaining the course.

Course development cost	$100,000
Lifespan of the course (years)	4
Amortized development cost	$25,000
(development cost/lifespan)	
Course offering cost	$15,000
Total cost	$40,000

After adding up the costs, Kevin is not daunted by the $40,000 annual cost for each course he develops and offers. To calculate profit, Kevin subtracts expenses from revenues:

Annual revenue	$50,000
Annual expenses	$40,000
Annual profit	$10,000

For each course, Kevin estimates a $10,000 profit, or a profit margin of 25 percent. Such a profit margin is not spectacular, but 25 percent is better than some of his dot-com investments did back in 1999.

Playing around with this simple model, Kevin realizes some economic truths about e-learning. Success requires keeping development costs low and attracting an adequate number of learners who are willing to pay a sufficient price to take the course. If you want to experiment with this model, you can download a spreadsheet from this book's companion Website at www.horton.com/leading.

How Much Can You Charge for Courses?

One of the questions most often asked by internal and external consultants about e-learning is, "How should we price e-learning courses?" Unfortunately there is no standard, established pricing model. A quick search on the Web finds seemingly equivalent courses varying in cost by a factor of 10 or 20. Here are some suggestions for how to price your offering realistically:

- *Conduct a market survey.* How much do others charge for e-learning courses of the same duration, general subject matter, and quality level as those you plan to offer? Even if the range is wide, you can at least bracket your assumptions. If you are introducing a new course in an already highly competitive market, you may find it difficult to charge at the high end of the price range.
- *Use established forms as a baseline.* Survey the general difference in prices between classroom and e-learning offerings on the same subject. If you charge $400 per day for your classroom training and the e-learning courses in your area of expertise go for about 20 percent of the cost of their classroom equivalents, then price your e-learning course at $80.
- *Add visible value.* To charge an above-average price for your e-learning, it must offer some perceived premium value. If you are the leading expert on a subject or if your conventional training classes have won quality awards, you may be able to leverage this reputation in the e-learning world.

How Can E-Learning Boost Other Revenue Sources?

Rather than depend on e-learning as a direct source of revenue, you may choose to use it to enhance other revenue streams. Try these ideas:

- *Advertise and promote your expertise.* Offer a free or low-cost e-learning course to publicize your expertise to a broader audience than you can reach solely through conventional means.
- *Steer learners to higher-margin courses.* Use e-learning courses to whet learners' appetites for your more substantial and more profitable classroom courses.
- *Merchandise your books, tapes, and other products.* If a high percentage of your profit comes from the sales of books, tapes, and other materials related to your training, use e-learning to lead learners to your e-commerce store.
- *Promote your custom consulting services.* E-learning can relieve consultants and instructors from repetitive teaching chores, freeing them for more lucrative, custom consulting work. Use e-learning courses to teach routine subjects and reveal your expertise to potential clients of your consulting services.
- *Hire virtual trainers.* If you are having trouble hiring instructors to teach routine courses, use e-learning to teach those courses, thereby freeing instructors for more advanced and profitable courses.

YOUR TURN

How do the ideas in this chapter apply to you and your organization? In other words, what's in it for your organization (WIIFYO)? The following assessments will help you find out. (Just a reminder: If you do not want to write in this book, you can download copies of all the "Your Turn" activities from the book's companion Website, www.horton.com/leading.)

Determine the primary benefits that e-learning offers your organization. Consider the ways that e-learning can save or make money for your organization, and list them in worksheet 3-1.

Worksheet 3-1. How can your organization benefit from e-learning?		
Possible E-Learning Application	**Money Saver? (✔)**	**Money Maker? (✔)**

Now, using the example shown in this chapter as a model, compare costs for one of your classroom courses with an e-learning alternative (worksheet 3-2).

The next step, of course, is to compute a business model. Imagine that you must use e-learning to generate a profit. Perhaps you are a stand-alone training organization or your department must operate as a profit center within a larger organization. Based on the example from this chapter, calculate the business results for a hypothetical project with worksheet 3-3.

Worksheet 3-2. Compare costs of classroom and e-learning courses for your organization.

Costs for Course Development

	Classroom	E-learning
Development cost per day of training		
× Days of training		
= Total development costs		

Costs for Offering Training

	Classroom	E-learning
Classroom facilities		
+ Instructor time		
+ Web server		
= Total offering costs		

Costs Due to Learners

	Classroom	E-learning
Travel		
+ Lost profit		
+ Technical support		
= Total per learner		
× Number of learners		
= Total costs due to learners		

The Bottom Line (Total Costs)

	Classroom	E-learning
Total development costs		
+ Total offering costs		
+ Total costs due to learners		
= Total costs		

Worksheet 3-3. Apply a business model for e-learning at your organization.

Revenue		
	Amount	
Enrollment fee		$ per learner
× Number of learners		learners per year
= Total revenue		$ per year

Expenses		
	Amount	
Course development costs		$
÷ Life span of the course		years
= Amortized development costs		$ per year
+ Course offering costs		$ per year
= Total expenses		$ per year

Profit		
	Amount	
Revenue		$ per year
− Expenses		$ per year
= Profit		$ per year

Did you make money? Enough?

4

Where Should I Target E-Learning?

No form of training, especially one as new as e-learning, is ideal for all purposes. As you move your organization toward e-learning, pick projects that benefit from what e-learning offers. Consider the kinds of projects and types of learning that can benefit most from e-learning.

WHY NOT JUST REPLACE CLASSROOM TRAINING?

One obvious target for e-learning is existing classroom training. Many managers new to e-learning try to use it to replace successful but expensive classroom-training programs. Such a strategy may yield a net gain but miss greater opportunities. The most cost-effective application of e-learning may not be to replace classroom training, but to bring training to those who cannot or will not take classroom training (figure 4-1).

Figure 4-1. Expanding the universe of learning in your organization.

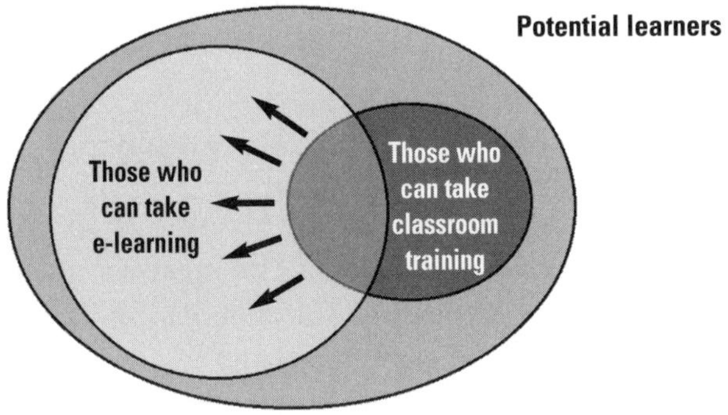

The fundamental problem with classrooms is not that they do not work, but that they do not work for everyone. Who are the people who cannot or will not take classroom training?

Well, they are those whose job duties rule out classroom training. These include those who work far from the site of training and have limited time or funds for travel. Others in this category are the people too busy to accommodate the fixed schedule of classroom training. Either they cannot be off their jobs that long or cannot free up the specific dates of classroom training. Some busy workers need training now and cannot wait for an opening in a scheduled training class. The pace and pressures of business are making classroom training a less desirable option.

Another group of people ripe for another solution are the ones who find understanding and communicating in the classroom difficult. Learners with even a slight hearing loss may have difficulty understanding the instructor. So, too, will second-language learners. The problem may be compounded by an instructor who speaks in a heavy accent, mumbles, or uses a great deal of slang. Visual impairments, even a common one like nearsightedness, can make reading handwritten notes or small type difficult or impossible. Speech impairments or self-consciousness may inhibit learners from speaking out in class. The asynchronous, anonymous nature of e-learning, combined with the use of redundant media, can overcome many of these difficulties. Learners can pick media that suit their abilities and read or listen at their own pace. Shy people who find face-to-face interaction very difficult may find empowerment in the faceless environment of e-learning.

A third group to consider are those barred from classroom training by economic barriers. Even if training is free, many corporate departments flinch at the travel and time-off-the-job costs required to send their employees to distant classroom training. These concerns are even greater for the vast armies of self-employed contractors and independent consultants who must bear the full costs of training themselves. Any option that lowers the total cost of training will benefit this group.

Ask yourself, "Of all the people I should be training, how many need an alternative to my current ways of delivering training?" In targeting e-learning, we should consider its potential to serve these neglected groups.

WHAT ARE THE EASY TARGETS?

One strategy for initially deploying e-learning is to pick projects with the highest odds of success. Just look for the most successful uses of e-learning and pick similar projects. For example, e-learning has proven quite adept at teaching factual information to learners who already have Web or intranet access and who are located in more than three separate cities. If your project matches these criteria, then the odds for e-learning success are high because such projects take full advantage of the power of e-learning while avoiding its difficulties.

PICK YOUR GOALS

E-learning is not a panacea. It can accomplish bold objectives. It can achieve impressive advances. Nevertheless, it cannot do everything at once, especially on a limited budget within a reasonable timeframe. To use e-learning effectively, you have to focus on what matters to your organization. To that end, spend some time sharpening your focus and calibrating the expectations of your organization. For your first few e-learning projects, pick one or two of these goals—no more:

- saving money on the training you already offer
- making money selling training content
- offering training to a wider audience
- improving the quality and effectiveness of training
- shortening the time required to train large groups of people
- improving transfer of learning to workplace performance.

WHAT SHOULD YOU CONSIDER WHEN DECIDING?

Choosing between conventional training and e-learning is often a complex decision. You must weigh many factors. Use the following sections as a checklist as you consider your specific situation.

Characteristics of Learners

Learning must fit the needs and abilities of learners. Consider the characteristics listed in table 4-1 as you evaluate your potential learners. Remember that neither form of training is perfect for all learners or even for any individual learner. You must decide which characteristics of learners most affect learning in your situation and choose accordingly.

Economics

If cost is no object, you can use any form of training you want. If financial resources and expectations limit your choice of training approach, consider these issues carefully using table 4-2. Consider carefully how each of these objectives applies to your situation and your goals.

Table 4-1. Comparing learner requirements for classroom training and e-learning.

Characteristic	Conventional Classroom Training	E-Learning
Value of Learners' Time	Learners must commit to a fixed schedule and may have to spend time traveling to the site of training.	Learners can better fit training into work schedules. No travel is required.
Motivation	Instructors and peers can motivate learners. Highly motivated learners, however, may feel constrained.	High levels of self-motivation are required for e-learning. Highly motivated individuals can proceed at their own pace.
Language Skills	Learners must have effective listening and reading skills.	Learners can listen to or read material again. Multimedia lessens dependence on language.
Computer Skills	No computer skills are required.	Learners must have basic computer-operations and Web-navigation skills. They may have to learn new collaboration tools as well.
Physical Abilities	Participation in classroom learning is limited by visual, hearing, and motion impairments.	Properly designed e-learning when combined with assistive technologies can provide training for those with common disabilities.

Table 4-2. Cost comparisons for classroom training and e-learning.

Issue	Conventional Classroom Training	E-Learning
Budget	Will require a large ongoing budget for delivery.	Developing or purchasing training will require a large up-front investment
Development Time	Development is quick and simple and requires only a knowledgeable instructor supported by simple audiovisual materials.	Development time may be significant, especially if multimedia presentations or high degrees of interactivity are required.
Availability of Experts	Requires a high ratio of trainers to learners.	The expertise of a few can be made available to many.
Computer and Telecommunications Technology	No special technology required.	For multimedia, learners require a powerful computer and a fast communications link.
Travel Costs	Travel costs are high if learners or trainers must travel for training.	No travel is required.

Subject of Training

Some subjects are easier to teach by e-learning than others are. Some can be taught entirely by e-learning, but others require a combination of e-learning and conventional techniques. Consider carefully the kinds of learning experiences necessary to teach your subject and the best way to effect those experiences (table 4-3).

Characteristics of the Subject Matter

Certain subject matters require special handling because of their perishable or proprietary nature. Classroom and e-learning environments vary in their ability to meet the requirements these characteristics impose. Before committing to e-learning, consider some of the critical characteristics of the knowledge or skills you must teach (table 4-4).

Table 4-3. Suitability of subject matter for classroom training or e-learning.

Subject	Conventional Classroom Training	E-Learning
Knowledge Training	Using instructors to teach knowledge, especially rote or routine knowledge, is not efficient.	E-learning can efficiently and reliably teach straightforward knowledge subjects.
Soft Skills and Leadership Skills	Classroom meetings are effective for subjects that depend on face-to-face contact to observe tone of voice, facial expressions, body language, and gestures.	E-learning may require multimedia and collaboration technologies for teaching these subjects.
Psychomotor Skills	Direct observation of learner's physical movements is easy in the classroom.	E-learning can demonstrate psychomotor skills but not easily evaluate student performance.
Attitude Training	Group activities in a classroom can reveal attitudes and allow the instructor to monitor changes.	Simulated social environments can motivate change. Online group activities require collaboration technologies.
Operator Training	Instructors can monitor performance on actual equipment.	Expensive simulators may be required but practice is not limited by equipment availability.
Safety Training	Instructors can guide learners through dangerous activities.	Self-directed training in dangerous activities can be risky. Simulations, however, can let learners experience the negative consequences of dangerous behavior.

**Table 4-4. Characteristics of subject matter that impinge
on choice of classroom training or e-learning.**

Characteristic	Conventional Classroom Training	E-Learning
Security or Confidentiality	Training can be restricted to secure facilities.	Secure computer systems and links are required.
Certification or Accreditation Requirements	Instructors routinely monitor testing and performance.	Testing can be automated but positively identifying the remote test-taker may prove difficult. Human proctors may be necessary.
Urgency	Because classroom training can be developed quickly, it is suited for short-term training needs.	Subjects with long-term needs can pay back the additional development required for e-learning.
Stability	Updating a course requires retraining instructors and revising materials. Learners may have to retake the course.	Materials can be revised in place. Refresher microcourses can be provided to geographically scattered learners.

Style of Delivery

If training is to support organizational goals, that training must fit into a matrix of related organizational activities and processes. That fit can depend on the way training is delivered and how training relates to other corporate activities. Consider issues of how your organization wants to deliver training (table 4-5).

Training Media and Methods

Certain subjects and certain learning goals require specific media or training methods, either because these are the most effective or because learners are more accustomed to these media and methods. Consider how each approach helps you meet your learning objectives (table 4-6).

Table 4-5. How classroom training and e-learning can help achieve your organizational goals.

Issue	Conventional Classroom Training	E-Learning
Global Delivery	Scheduling and delivering training around the world may be expensive and time consuming.	Training can be made available globally as soon as it is developed.
Consistency	The quality and effectiveness of training depends on the instructor.	All learners receive the same quality of instruction. Any improvements apply to all subsequent offerings.
Data Collection and Tracking	Manual, paper-based methods are time consuming and expensive.	Data can be automatically recorded to a database and analyzed instantly—with the appropriate software, of course.
Access to Reference Materials	Paper handouts are cumbersome for instructors and learners.	Large amounts of materials can be posted to a Website. Courses can link to material elsewhere on the Web.
Availability at Time of Need	Learners must wait for a training class to be offered.	Self-directed e-learning can begin at any time.

Table 4-6. Meeting your objectives through different media and methods.

Medium or Method	Conventional Classroom Training	E-Learning
Audio	Instructors can play audiotapes in class.	Learners require a moderate-speed connection, but they can replay the audio as necessary.
Video	Instructors can play videotapes in class.	Learners require a high-speed connection. They can, however, replay the video as necessary.
Collaboration and Teamwork	Team activities are simple and direct in the classroom.	Teamwork requires collaborative technologies.
Discussion	Seminar settings make conversation natural.	E-learning requires chat rooms and discussion forums for effective discussion.

YOUR TURN

At least half the success of e-learning depends on your choice of target. What are the best uses for e-learning in your organization? Use worksheet 4-1 to determine the best first targets for e-learning in your organization. (If you do not want to mark up this book, download copies of these worksheets from the book's companion Website www.horton.com/leading.)

Worksheet 4-1. List some easy targets for e-learning in your organization.

To Teach What?	To Whom?

For your most pressing training need, analyze the suitability of classroom training and e-learning. In worksheet 4-2, list all the relevant factors and weigh the costs and benefits of each approach. Which did you pick and why?

Identify groups of people who need knowledge and skills but do not take training offered by your organization, and suggest ways e-learning might help reach these people. Use worksheet 4-3 to identify who's missing.

Worksheet 4-2. Tame your wildest problem.

What is your most pressing training need?	
List some advantages of using classroom training to meet this need.	List some advantages of using e-learning to meet this need.
Which is the better choice? Why?	

Worksheet 4-3. Find ways to reach new audiences with e-learning.		
Who does not take the training they need?	**Why do they not take training?**	**How could e-learning meet their training needs?**

5

How Can You Sell E-Learning?

To persuade your organization to invest in e-learning, you must convince key individuals who will make the decision to adopt or reject e-learning. Some of these individuals are within your organization; others are not. All of them will demand to know what e-learning offers them and those they represent. Let's see how to plan your sales campaign, dispel the hype and hysteria around e-learning, make its advantages clear, and suggest solutions for its disadvantages.

TO WHOM MUST YOU SELL E-LEARNING?

To steer your organization to e-learning, you must convince important decision makers that e-learning is the right approach. And just who are these decision makers?

The first person to convince is you. Do you objectively and honestly believe that e-learning is the best approach for your organization and its learners? If not, recommend some other solution. No reasonable person claims that e-learning is always the best solution. Keep an open mind and consider blended solutions.

Next, you must convince the producers of training. These are usually the heads and senior staff of departments conducting classroom training now. You may also need to convince anyone up the chain of command with authority over budgets, schedules, and staffing assignments. Bring classroom instructors into the loop to alleviate any feelings that their jobs and job satisfaction are threatened by e-learning.

You must also enlist the support and assistance of your IT department. The IT staff may have responsibility for the technical infrastructure needed to deliver e-learning in your organization.

Finally, you must convince consumers of training that e-learning will meet their varied needs. Consumers of training include both the learners who take the training and the managers who purchase or approve enrollment in the training.

How Can You Convince Them?

Selling e-learning is like selling anything else. You must convince the buyer that your product meets their financial, intellectual, and emotional needs. Make clear the WIIFM ("what's in it for me?"). And, remember that even management committees are made up of individuals, each with idiosyncratic viewpoints, prejudices, and concerns.

Some ways of communicating the WIIFMs include the following:

- ROI analyses showing the economic value of e-learning
- live demonstrations of e-learning products
- sample e-learning courses
- written reports highlighting the advantages of e-learning
- testimonials from satisfied learners and their managers
- statistics of successful applications of e-learning in situations similar to your own.

Selling to Producers of Training

Producers of training are those who create and deploy training and education. These can include internal training departments; colleges and universities; and independent, for-profit training firms. Producers are highly concerned with the economics of developing and delivering training.

For producers of training, e-learning offers cost savings and efficiency. To sell e-learning, feature these advantages:

- lower costs for facilities, including classrooms, break rooms, instructor offices, and libraries
- lower costs for instructors because a "facilitator" can oversee the e-learning of many more learners than a classroom instructor can
- reduced travel by instructors resulting in lower costs and happier instructors
- reduced administrative costs due to automated registration, ordering, billing, tracking, and evaluation
- greater opportunities to reuse training materials once developed and perfected
- ease of updating and revising courses in place
- enhanced reputation of the producer as innovative, financially responsible, and technically savvy.

Despite these significant advantages, the newness of e-learning and a lack of experience with it raises several concerns for developers of training. Table 5-1 lists some of the main concerns and ways to overcome these concerns.

Selling to Consumers of Training

Consumers of training include the actual learners who take the training and their managers who approve or authorize the training. Among the advantages that e-learning can provide for consumers are the following:

- E-learning is potentially more convenient, economical, and effective than other forms of training.
- Learners can take training at convenient times and locations.
- Learners control the pace and content of training, thereby customizing it to their needs and preferred learning styles.
- Learners do not have to travel to take training, saving time and money.
- Appropriately designed multimedia presentations help overcome common visual, hearing, language, and physical disabilities.
- Learning is more efficient. Learners may require less time to learn the same material.
- Learning is less stressful. Learners can take their time answering questions, can repeat material as necessary, and do not feel unfairly judged for irrelevant factors such as their accent or appearance.

Table 5-1. Producers' concerns about e-learning and possible solutions.

Concern	Solution
The economics of e-learning are unproven. Costs are hard to predict. Revenues are even harder to predict.	Target e-learning selectively. Pick projects with the highest probability of economic success.
It is difficult to authenticate remote learners during testing.	For certification testing, use public proctors, such as librarians, for final exams.
E-learning requires mastering new tools, technologies, and techniques.	Emphasize that such knowledge and skills are an investment and will be recovered over many future projects.
Low-speed connections may limit the use of multimedia.	Focus on interactivity rather than glitzy presentations. Use multimedia conservatively and only where it really contributes to learning.
Existing classroom instructors may feel that their jobs are threatened or that they will be forced into jobs for which they are ill suited.	Educate trainers in e-learning techniques. Point out new career opportunities in e-learning. Reassure them that classrooms will not soon vanish.

Of course, e-learning is new to many consumers. It may seem strange and foreboding. Getting started may take more effort than some are willing to spend (table 5-2).

Speak the Language of Business

You promise to switch from one-size-fits-all, just-in-case courses to just-in-time modules that are tailored to individual learners. The board of directors looks bored. You tell them how you are replacing obsolete didactic paradigms with empowering, constructive ones. Three members actually yawn. You describe the active learning experience made possible by multimedia. The chief executive officer asks how much all this multimedia stuff is going to cost. You display charts showing improved retention and transfer rates in your prototype project. The chairman of the board thanks you for your time and says the board has other proposals to evaluate.

When selling your ideas for e-learning to business managers, couch your proposal in terms that directly demonstrate the benefits to the business. It is your responsibility, not theirs, to translate proposed training advances into promises of business results.

Table 5-2. Consumers' concerns and possible solutions.

Concern	Solution
E-learning provides little face-to-face contact.	Use collaborative technologies (e-mail, discussion groups, chat) to enable social interaction. Point out that some e-learners have reported better contacts with their peers and instructor than in classroom courses (Cooper, 1999; Docent, 1999; Schutte, 1997).
E-learners must master new technologies.	Simplify the technologies and provide help for learning them. Point out that mastery of these technologies is a valuable job skill in its own right.
Technologies that support e-learning are expensive.	Design your e-learning to work on the computers people already have. Show that an investment in e-learning technologies has benefits beyond training as well.
E-learning requires greater self-motivation.	Explicitly motivate learners. Have them commit to a learning schedule and follow-up. Make learning fun. Clearly recognize and reward progress. Continually remind learners of the value of what they are learning.
E-learning must compete with job duties and a busy life.	Design e-learning in short, self-contained modules that fit into a busy schedule. Set up quiet e-learning centers where workers can take e-learning courses away from their desks and telephones.

What kind of business results do managers and executives appreciate and understand—and that e-learning can deliver? Here are the kinds of promises that will sell e-learning to business leaders.

- E-learning will reduce the total cost of training by 60 percent through reductions in time off the job, travel expenses, and lost sales.
- With e-learning, you will be able to launch the new product line six weeks earlier with a fully trained salesforce, thereby adding a full six weeks of sales.
- E-learning will reduce manufacturing costs by 18 percent by cutting workers' time to productivity from four weeks to one week, by reducing errors and rework by 12 percent, and cutting line stoppages from an average of 20 minutes to just five minutes.
- E-learning will double sales of high-margin products without having to take the salesforce out of the field or retraining.
- E-learning will reduce calls to customer support to answer simple procedural questions by 6,000 calls per month, thereby achieving savings of $180,000 monthly and increasing customer satisfaction.

Mentally rehearse your presentation before an imaginary audience of skeptical, cynical business managers who know nothing about training except that it consumes a large budget. What can you say that will make these hardened business leaders smile and nod at one another?

SELL REALITY TO REPLACE HYPE

Sometimes your job as an e-learning advocate will be to correct unrealistic hopes for e-learning. In this case you do not want to dampen enthusiasm about e-learning, just recalibrate expectations to something that can be achieved by mortals.

Your first step should be to see the depth and breadth of the delusion. How strongly does the person hold to unrealistic expectations and how many others suffer under this same delusion? It is one thing if one middle manager believes e-learning will solve all training problems and quite another if the entire executive corps and board of directors suffer from the same mass delusion.

The next step may be to probe for defensiveness. Do the deluded souls seem open to new facts or do they react as if you are telling them the love of their lives is an axe murderer? If the former, a well-researched white paper or presentation can do the job. If the latter, you must go more slowly and gently.

Strongly held misconceptions seldom yield to a frontal assault. You must seduce deluded managers into revising their opinions. (Here's an opportunity to put all that learning theory you studied to the test.) Perhaps you could suggest performing a more detailed analysis of how e-learning will affect your particular organization. Ensure that the analysis includes some of the risks and drawbacks of e-learning, such as its high up-front development costs, its novelty for many learners, and its dependence on a technological infrastructure. If possible, build a financial model as a spreadsheet that everyone can use to perform what-if analyses to see the consequences of varying assumptions. Participants in the study may be driven to the conclusion that, yes, e-learning can do wonderful things—but only with highly optimistic assumptions.

A second approach may be to suggest a pilot project to record and demonstrate the wonderful benefits of e-learning. Keep the pilot project small enough that it does not endanger essential corporate activities, and document it thoroughly: costs, resources required, reactions of learners, improvements in job performance, and overall ROI.

The advantage of both these approaches is that they take time. Time itself may cool irrational ardor for e-learning and open the mind for the results of the analysis or pilot project. Those results will then paint a realistic picture of the benefits and costs of e-learning.

OUR TURN: SELLING RESULTS, NOT ILLUSIONS

Selling e-learning requires setting positive, yet realistic, expectations. As e-learning consultants, we sometimes find ourselves having to convince clients to forego e-learning or to drastically scale down their e-learning projects. Often clients are convinced that creating and selling e-learning is a sure way to make vast sums of money. They have heard all the hype. If they build it, learners will come—and pay.

We recently worked with a small project-management company. A good portion of the company's income came from providing in-house classroom training to other companies and organizations. To augment the stand-up training and meet the needs of some of their customers, the company wanted to create a Web-based version of their standard one-week course. The principals also saw e-learning as a way of enhancing their visibility and credibility, thereby increasing their consulting practice as well as boosting demand for their advanced classroom courses.

We came into this project after the clients had received a bid to do the entire course with Macromedia's Flash animation tool. After the sticker shock, they called us for a consultation. What we realized after our first meeting was that they didn't really know what producing e-learning entails. Neither of the principals had ever taken a Web-based course nor did they understand the basic technology involved. All they had to go on was the information they had received from suppliers at numerous e-learning conferences. Our job, then, was to explain the process in enough detail so that they could make a sound business decision on whether e-learning was the path to take.

One of the first things we did was take them through a spreadsheet for a typical training provider (the business model presented in chapter 3). The biggest surprise was the large, up-front cost for development in contrast with the small price they might reasonably charge per learner. They quickly realized that to recoup their investment and make a profit, they would need to move hundreds of learners through the course each year. To ensure that level of enrollment would require a great deal of marketing and even more luck.

Our clients were pretty discouraged after this first meeting. Although they still really wanted to enhance their business by offering an e-learning alternative, they couldn't make the ROI calculations work in their favor. We suggested an alternative approach.

Because two of their objectives were to increase their consulting business and create a market for their more advanced (and expensive) classroom courses, we suggested that they look at e-learning as a marketing tool. Instead of diving right in and developing a whole course, why not develop a small lesson module on a topic of broad interest to managers and offer it free from their Website?

This mini-course could do double—even triple—duty. First, potential clients viewing it could get a taste of the quality of our clients' training and the breadth of their expertise. Second, it could be assigned as prework for the classroom course. Finally, it would let them get their foot in the e-learning door without a large initial investment. As a bonus, many of the up-front development activities, such as deciding on the look and feel of their e-learning, developing page templates, and establishing a standard organization would already be done for subsequent modules.

This is the approach our clients took. E-learning is still one of their long-term business goals. However, because they are a small company with limited time, money, and human resources, they see the need to move slowly and build demand before they commit those limited resources to a full-scale course development effort.

Your Turn

Even great ideas need passionate advocates. How will you sell e-learning to the decision makers in your organization? How will you overcome the objections of skeptics and pessimists?

First, try to anticipate reactions. Think back on the e-learning you have taken and how it differed from traditional training. Then answer the questions posed in worksheet 5-1.

Within your organization, identify the persons or groups crucial to the success of e-learning and plan how you will overcome their concerns (worksheet 5-2).

For each of the sales tactics mentioned in the chapter, how will you use it to sell e-learning within your organization? Feel free to add some sales tactics of your own. Plan your sales tactics using worksheet 5-3.

Worksheet 5-1. Anticipating the benefits and challenges of e-learning in your organization.

Difference Between E-Learning and Traditional Training	Possible Benefits of the E-Learning Difference for Your Organization	Possible Obstacles of the E-Learning Difference for Your Organization

Worksheet 5-2. Developing a sales plan for e-learning in your organization.

Person or Group	Primary Concern of the Person or Group	How to Satisfy This Concern

Worksheet 5-3. Using sales tactics to sell e-learning in your organization.

Sales Tactic	How to Apply Within Your Organization
ROI Analyses	
Live Demonstrations	
Sample E-Learning Courses	
Reports Highlighting Advantages of E-Learning	
Testimonials From Satisfied Learners and Their Managers	
Statistics of Successful Applications	

6

What Kinds of E-Learning Can You Create?

E-learning comes in many forms. In chapter 1, e-learning was defined as using Internet and digital technologies to create educational experiences for people. These technologies include Webpages, interactive displays, electronic documents, animation and video sequences, email, chat and instant messaging, discussion forums, videoconferencing, screen-sharing, online white boards, and others. These technologies can be combined in many combinations to create different forms of e-learning.

One of your earliest and most important decisions will be which of these forms you want to create. Let's look at some common forms of e-learning and where you may want to use them. Remember that these are not all of the possible forms, just a sample of the most common ones. We have formatted this chapter a bit differently to make it easier for you to compare these alternatives.

Self-Directed Web-Based Training

Self-directed Web-based training (WBT) aims to use the Internet to deliver high-quality learning experiences to independent learners. Content consists of Webpages, multimedia presentations, and other interactive learning experiences housed and maintained on a Web server (figure 6-1). The materials are accessed through a Web browser.

So far the experience is not unlike that of taking a computer-based training (CBT) course from a CD-ROM. Where this approach goes beyond CBT is in the potential to track learners' actions in a central database and the ability to access the riches of the Internet.

Using Self-Directed Web-Based Training

Consider self-directed WBT for subjects that can be learned alone by independent learners who want to follow their own schedule. You may also need to adopt this form when your course must work both from the Web and CD-ROM, for example, when learners lack continuous network connections.

Keep in mind, though, that independent learners can be lonely learners. Add extra doses of motivation and feedback. Monitor the progress of learners to pre-empt dropouts. Provide at least an email address for getting help.

Figure 6-1. Self-directed Web-based training.

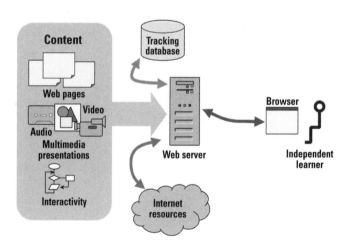

50

FACILITATED WEB-BASED TRAINING

Facilitated Web-based training melds the advantages of self-directed WBT and classroom training. Like self-directed WBT, facilitated Web-based training caters to the needs of learners who cannot conform to the rigid schedule of classroom training. To the structure of self-directed WBT, it adds a facilitator (figure 6-2).

The facilitator is not an instructor in disguise. The facilitator does not directly conduct learning events or try to wrest control from the learners. The facilitator answers learners' questions and helps solve problems.

> ## Using Facilitated Web-Based Training
>
> **W**here should you use facilitated Web-based training? Facilitated Web-based training provides maximum flexibility and long-term economy. However, it is best suited for independent and motivated learners, and it requires a significant up-front investment for the complex infrastructure needed.
>
> The key ingredient in this form of e-learning is the facilitator. This is not an easy role to fill. It requires balancing the goal of self-directed learning with the need to help learners who are not being as productive as pos-sible. For economic reasons, you want the facilitator to handle as many learners as possible without denying any learners the attention they need.

Learners may communicate with the facilitator through email, through scheduled chat sessions or telephone calls, and through messages posted on a course discussion forum.

Figure 6-2. Facilitated Web-based training.

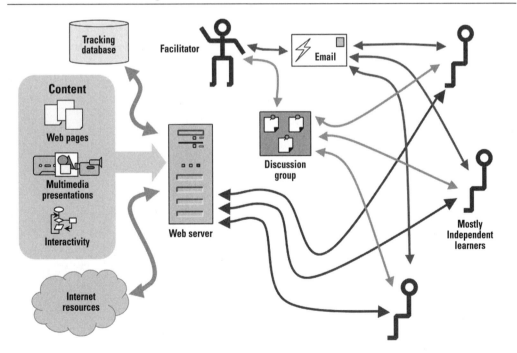

WEB-CONDUCTED CLASSROOM COURSE

One form of e-learning uses Web technologies to open the enrollment of conventional training classes to include distant learners. Such classes typically use a videoconferencing facility to Webcast lectures, demonstrations, and other live classroom activities through a streaming-media server (figure 6-3).

Using Web-Conducted Classroom Courses

When should you use Web-conducted classes? Consider them for subjects that require live demonstrations or the emotional impact of a human instructor. And, use them for learners who need the familiar structure and discipline of classroom training. You may also use them when you do not have the time or the budget to prepare effective interactive materials required for facilitated WBT. They are great for light-duty training, such as briefing a distributed salesforce on the features of a new product.

Such courses look seductively easy: Just step in front of the camera and talk. The resulting talking-head lectures only serve to point out the need for proper preparation. Rehearse, review, and rehearse again. Record presentations and experience them from the learner's viewpoint. And, remember to send copies of graphics and other referenced materials to learners ahead of time.

Web-conducted classroom courses typically provide a back channel so that learners can ask questions. Such a channel may be implemented by letting learners type their questions into a chat window or send them in by email. If all learners have fast connections, the back channel may use audio or video capabilities. A telephone line is another option. Assignments are typically made by posting them to a class discussion forum where learners can also post their completed homework.

This structure will seem familiar to learners because it has the same artifacts and expectations as the form of training they have experienced most of their lives. It requires the least effort to convert ma-terials. Materials can simply be held in front of the video camera, or they can be scanned in. However, much material does not work when filtered through the medium of Internet video, and few instructors have experience teaching remotely.

Figure 6-3. Web-conducted classroom course.

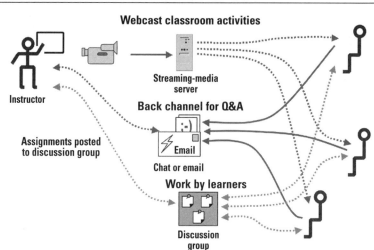

EMAIL CORRESPONDENCE COURSE

Email correspondence courses update the venerable postal correspondence course. The course is simplicity itself. An instructor sends an assignment to the learner who completes and returns it. The instructor then critiques the learner's work and returns the graded assignment (figure 6-4). This cycle can repeat as many times as necessary.

Email correspondence courses are not limited to exchanges of brief, unformatted text messages. Keep in mind that today most email software can display HTML formatting and that email messages can contain other file formats as attachments. If you are considering an email correspond-ence course, consider discussion group seminars as well. Though a bit more complex, discussion group seminars offer more opportunities for group interaction.

Using Email Correspondence Courses

Where would you use email correspondence courses? Of all the forms of e-learning, email correspondence courses require the least technology and are the simplest and quickest to implement. Learners who can hit the reply button in their email menus have the necessary skills. Email correspondence courses are effective for teaching material that requires critique of work done by individual learners but not face-to-face contact. They are best for subjects that can be conveyed in text and simple graphics. However, with fast network connections, email courses can contain multimedia attachments.

The critical element in email correspondence courses is the feedback provided by the instructor. The feedback must be clear, polite, and complete. And it must be timely. Learners may take six weeks to complete an assignment, but they will inspect the instructor's comments on their submission immediately. Set clear expectations about the timing of feedback, say within three business days, and keep your promises.

Figure 6-4. Email correspondence course.

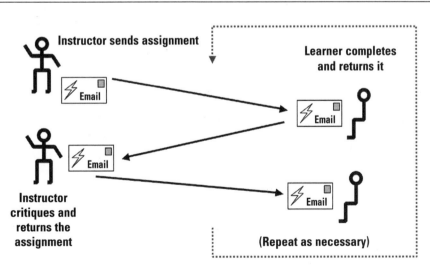

Instructor sends assignment

Learner completes and returns it

Email

Email

Email

Email

Instructor critiques and returns the assignment

(Repeat as necessary)

DISCUSSION GROUP SEMINARS

Another simple form of e-learning centers on use of online discussions. In such a scenario, the instructor posts an assignment to the discussion group (an Internet newsgroup or bulletin board) to which learners have access (figure 6-5). The assignment may include hyperlinks for assigned readings, individual or group activities for learners to perform, and other attached documents for use in the assignment.

Learners work individually or in teams to complete the assigned tasks. Then they post their work to the discussion group where the instructor and other learners may critique and discuss it.

Using Discussion Group Seminars

Discussion group seminars are most often used for subjects that do not require advanced multimedia but do rely upon collaboration, teamwork, and negotiation among multiple learners. If learner-to-learner interaction is more important than multimedia, a discussion group seminar is a good choice, especially if only slow or medium speed network connections are possible.

Apart from the discussion group software, which is relatively simple and inexpensive, the main requirement for discussion group seminars is a leader skilled in moderating online discussions. The leader must deftly steer discussions through controversial topics, encourage full participation, and tactfully settle disputes.

Figure 6-5. Online discussion group.

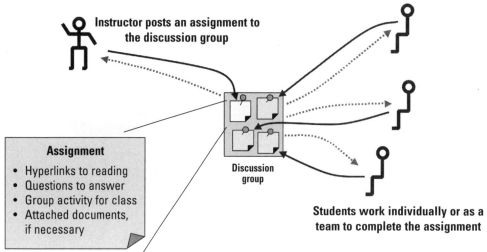

Instructor posts an assignment to the discussion group

Assignment
- Hyperlinks to reading
- Questions to answer
- Group activity for class
- Attached documents, if necessary

Discussion group

Students work individually or as a team to complete the assignment

GUIDED TOURS AND ONSCREEN WORKBOOKS

Guided tours and onscreen workbooks teach a complicated subject by leading the learner through the subject along a simple, predictable path, pointing out and commenting on important features along the way (figure 6-6).

In this example, a knowledge management system is equipped with a "tour" button. Clicking this button brings up a separate tour window containing a set of navigation buttons that take the learner through the most important parts of the knowledge management system. At each stop, important aspects are pointed out. Note that in this example, learners are encouraged to depart the tour and explore the stop on their own.

> ### Using Guided Tours and Onscreen Workbooks
>
> A guided tour or onscreen workbook may be a good fit if learners merely need an overview and a little encouragement to start exploring a subject on their own. By themselves, guided tours are seldom sufficient training on any complex subject, but may provide the orientation self-directed learners need to get started and may motivate them to seek out other forms of learning.
>
> The secret to a good guided tour is selectivity. A good tour includes the "key" stops, that is, the ones that unlock understanding of the whole. A guided tour that methodically covers every aspect of the subject may just leave learners lost in a maze of unconnected details.

They are also given instructions on how to find their own way to the next stop. Onscreen workbooks go further by giving learners explicit tasks to perform and by requiring them to enter the results in the workbook, which may be sent back to a facilitator or instructor.

Figure 6-6. Example of a "guided tour" through a knowledge management system.

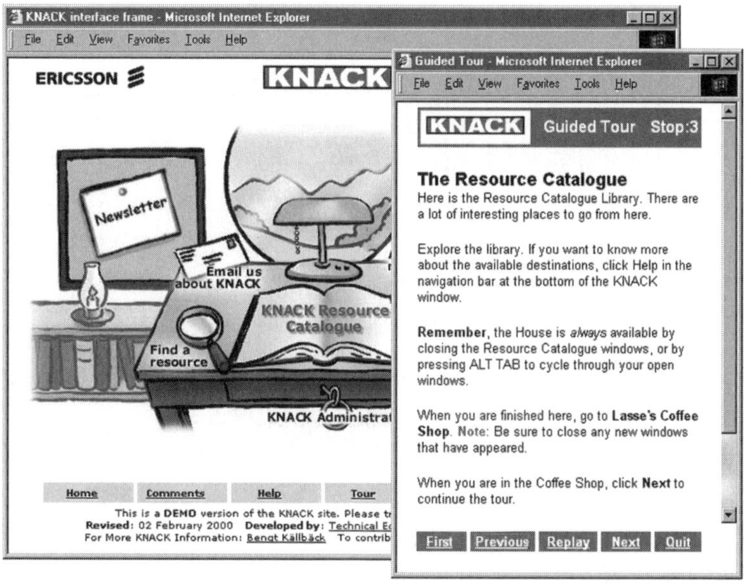

Source: Printed by permission of Ericsson Radio Systems AB and William Horton Consulting.

Learning Games

Another model infiltrating training and education is that of the computer game. Because computer games are often associated with play and violent imagery, educational purists have not yet recommended equipping learning workstations with joysticks. In fact, many have resisted the very idea that simple games and puzzles can be effective tools for learning. Nevertheless, as the second generation of computer game veterans moves into the workforce, more and more instructional designers are discovering that games, puzzles, and simulations are an effective way to make training familiar, fun, and highly effective.

> ### Using Learning Games
>
> **C**omputer simulations and games, which let learners discover concepts for themselves, work well for teaching complex subjects that cannot be reduced to specific rules. Game formats may work in your organization for learners who prefer to learn by experience— or who only learn by experience.
>
> Do not underestimate the cost of developing a good game. The effort required for programming the game and developing its media are just part of the cost. The largest and most important effort may be in translating the learning goals of the game into a rich array of potential interactions and then specifying the sequence and flow among them. Just drawing the flowchart may be the hardest part.

One way to use games is to style learning simulations as games. The Crimescene game, shown in figure 6-7, teaches interviewing skills in the context of a police interview of a witness to a bank robbery. By successfully interviewing the witness, the player will be able to solve the crime and win the game.

The Crimescene game is based on the old-style computer adventure games, going back to the era of medieval mainframes, when the computer would describe a scene and the player would then type in a command indicating how to proceed. Because the Crimescene game had to work over a slow modem, it contains few graphics and no multimedia. Yet, learners found it engaging and challenging. You can find a link to this game on this book's companion Website at www .horton.com/leading/.

Figure 6-7. Screenshot from a computer learning game.

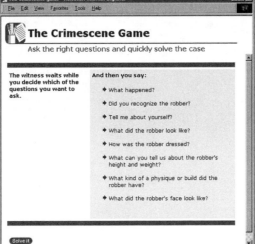

TELEMENTORING AND E-COACHING

The term mentor, referring to a sage advisor, goes back to the ancient Greeks. In Homer's *Odyssey,* when Odysseus leaves to sack Troy, he puts his son's education into the hands of a teacher named Mentor. Whenever the goddess Athena wishes to give the boy advice, she does so in the form of Mentor. Hence, the concept of a mentor has, from the beginning, meant a wiser person who provides guidance and advice. With advances in communication technologies, mentoring is possible on a much wider scale than ever before (figure 6-8). Mentor and protégé need not work in the same building or even on the same continent.

Some organizations are setting up formal telementoring or e-coaching programs. They use Web technologies to help match up mentors and protégés and to provide channels for communication. These channels include conferencing, chat, and email. Telementoring programs may also have an e-commerce component to compensate mentors even if only to ensure that mentors' efforts are made visible during their next performance appraisal. Such programs support long-term advisory relationships among professionals who may frequently change jobs and locations and whose schedules make regular face-to-face meetings impossible.

> ### Using Telementoring and E-Coaching
>
> Telementoring may be the answer if your organization needs to develop judgment and high-level thinking skills that cannot be reduced to the kind of rules and procedures that can be taught by other means. It is an important way of inducting new employees into the company culture. It can provide a valuable lifeline for employees struggling to balance creativity, tact, ambition, and ethics. Telementoring is especially valuable for employees who are separated from others in their field of expertise, for example, a field engineer assigned to assist a regional sales office.
>
> Telementoring requires matching the right mentor and protégé and establishing clear and realistic expectations for both parties. Recruiting and training potential mentors may be the first step. There are usually more protégés than qualified mentors. To clarify expectations, it may help to have participants develop a "contract" defining their respective responsibilities.

Figure 6-8. Prototype of a for-pay telementoring service.

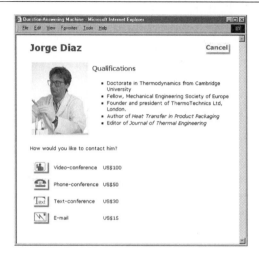

JOB AIDS

One often overlooked form of e-learning is the online job aid, which provides just-in-time knowledge in the form of immediate answers to specific questions. Job aids can take several forms. They can be sophisticated expert systems or just simple checklists. You can provide a glossary that allows people to look up the meaning of technical terms they encounter in their work. Or, you may provide a virtual consultant to guide them through a complex business decision, such as how to discipline an employee who has violated security regulations (figure 6-9).

Using Job Aids

Consider using online job aids in your organization for simple knowledge that must be applied at work. Use checklists to ensure workers consider all factors necessary to make a decision. Use simple procedures for common and critical tasks. Provide calculators to simplify the specific technical and business calculations workers are called on to perform. Craft virtual consultants for especially complex decisions.

You can use job aids to promote your training department. Distribute them freely, but be sure to include the logo of your training department and a hyperlink to a list of your training offerings.

The sample virtual consultant asks a few questions. Users answer the questions by selecting checkboxes, radio buttons, and other Webpage elements. The user then clicks on an "advise me" button and receives specific recommendations. The form also contains buttons to send a message immediately to the HR or legal department. You can link to this example from the companion Website for this book at www.horton.com/leading/.

Figure 6-9. Example of a "virtual consultant" job aid.

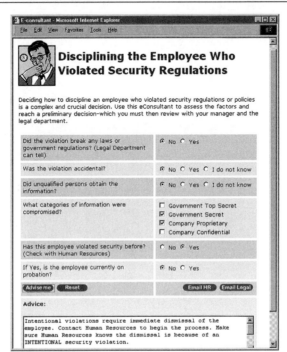

YOUR TURN

E-learning is more than electronic mimicry of classroom courses. E-learning can go beyond courses and current forms of learning. In designing your organization's e-learning solution, consider what forms of e-learning best meet your goals.

For a specific, course-sized learning goal, pick the best kind of e-learning to create. Write down three reasons to support your choice in worksheet 6-1.

For each type of e-learning, decide where it could best be used in your organization using worksheet 6-2.

Use the diagrams in this chapter and worksheet 6-3 to sketch a hybrid type of e-learning that combines the best features of two or more types of e-learning to solve a training problem experienced by your organization.

Worksheet 6-1. What type of e-learning should you use?		
Learning Goal	**Best-Suited E-Learning Type for This Goal**	**Reasons**
		1._____ 2._____ 3._____
		1._____ 2._____ 3._____
		1._____ 2._____ 3._____
		1._____ 2._____ 3._____
		1._____ 2._____ 3._____

Worksheet 6-2. Identify the best ways to apply different types of e-learning in your organization.

Type of E-Learning	Best Application in Your Organization
Self-directed Web-based training	
Facilitated Web-based training	
Web-conducted classroom course	
Email correspondence course	
Discussion group seminars	
Guided tours and onscreen workbooks	
Learning games and simulations	
Telementoring and e-coaching	
Job aids	

Worksheet 6-3. Combine types of e-learning to create a custom solution for your organization.

Learning Goal:

Sketch your e-learning solution based on the diagrams in this chapter.

7

Can You Blend E-Learning With Conventional Learning?

One problem of pitting e-learning against classroom training is that it suggests you must pick only one approach, thereby ignoring the possibilities of hybrid or blended forms. E-learning rewards open-minded pragmatists who look for ways to combine the best aspects of e-learning and conventional methods of training. Let's look at when, where, and how you may want to blend e-learning techniques with conventional classroom training.

OFFER PROVEN CLASSROOM MATERIALS

One way to enhance your overall training efforts by blending traditional and e-learning methods is to make your classroom materials available electronically. Such an offering is not a course. It is just course materials, but it's a start, and, for many who are hungry for learning, it is a virtual feast. For training organizations, it provides a way to begin building the skills, acceptance, and infrastructure they will need for true e-learning.

The first phase of this effort is to convert overheads to onscreen presentations—and make them legible and effective in that format. Once these onscreen presentations are working in the classroom, save a copy of the slides as HTML in Adobe Acrobat format. If practical, include notes to explain what the slides show (figure 7-1).

The next step is to capture the other components in electronic format. You can make audio or video recordings of the instructor. You can also convert the paper handouts and reading materials to some digital paper format, using Adobe Acrobat or some other program. Once you have all the materials in electronic form, you can organize them into a coherent package, which you can write onto CD-ROM so that learners can order it as well as put it on your server so learners can view it directly.

Figure 7-1. A first step toward e-learning: converting classroom material to electronic format.

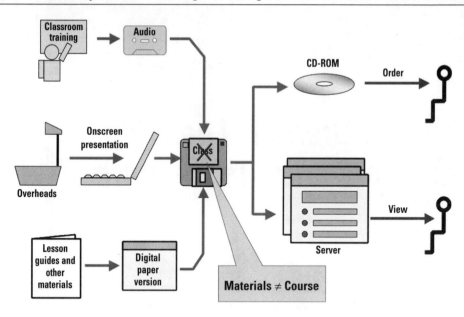

SERVE SANDWICHES

In blended learning methods, a sandwich involves neither bread nor peanut butter; it is a learning sequence in which one training medium precedes and follows another training medium.

Web-Classroom-Web Sandwich

The Web-classroom-Web sandwich surrounds a core of classroom training with Web-based introduction and follow-up (figure 7-2).

In this sandwich, the introductory Web-based material ensures that all learners are ready to take full advantage of the relatively short classroom sessions. The Web-based materials provide background and prerequisite material so that all learners fully understand the purpose of the course, that they all start with the same basic level of understanding, and that they all have the vocabulary required to discuss the subject. The classroom session, then, can consist of

Figure 7-2. Web-classroom-Web sandwich for blended learning.

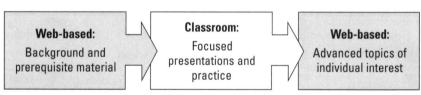

highly efficient, totally focused presentations and practice activities. The Web-based follow-up provides additional material on advanced subjects for learners who want to explore the subject further or who want additional practice.

Classroom-Web-Classroom Sandwich

The classroom-Web-classroom sandwich uses Web-based materials for its core but begins and ends with short classroom meetings (figure 7-3).

Figure 7-3. Classroom-Web-classroom sandwich for blended learning.

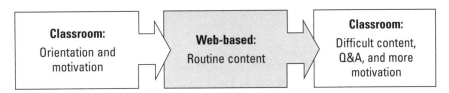

This combination begins with a brief face-to-face meeting of the learners, instructional designers, technical support staff, and facilitators for the course. The purpose of this meeting is to allay any concerns learners may have about the format of the course and to put a human face on the material that will follow.

The bulk of the content, especially routine knowledge, is presented in the middle of the sandwich using Web technologies. At the end, learners come together again. Here the facilitator can discuss difficult content and answer any questions learners may have.

The classroom-Web-classroom sandwich gently initiates learners into the world of e-learning. The beginning and ending classroom sessions supply the special motivation and support new e-learners need.

USE WEB CONTENT IN CLASSROOM TRAINING

With more than two billion Web pages available, it is a pretty dull instructional designer who cannot find at least some relevant Web-based material to incorporate into classroom training. Here are a few suggestions of Web resources that you can include in your classroom training:

- examples that illustrate the concepts you are teaching
- counter-examples that show the consequences of neglecting the concepts you are teaching
- scholarly papers on the subject you are teaching
- glossaries for the area of your course
- presentation slides and handouts on the subject of your course
- bibliographies on the subject of your course.

The easiest way to include such material is simply to link to them from a course home page available to learners. If you use PowerPoint slides in the classroom, you can include links on these slides to trigger the display of Web materials.

Add Internet Collaboration to Classroom Training

Almost every classroom course can benefit from better communication among participants. Table 7-1 lists a few ways you can incorporate Internet collaboration technologies into the framework of classroom training. Using such collaborative mechanisms in classroom training prepares learners for effective participation in e-learning.

Design Materials for Use in the Classroom and in E-Learning

One way to make your e-learning and classroom training more compatible, and save money at the same time, is to design your training materials so they can be used in both forms of training. For example, an animation that explains how your new payroll system works with your old sales-order system could be created in Macromedia's Flash and dropped onto Webpages for e-learning and onto Microsoft PowerPoint slides for use in the classroom.

The first step in such a "single-source" or "dual-use" strategy is to find out what media formats work in classroom training and in e-learning. For the classroom, you can just ask instructors and their managers. For e-learning, you must consider which browser and plug-ins learners already have—or can be coaxed into acquiring. (Chapter 9 will help you decide on technologies you can use.)

Table 7-1. Ways of integrating Internet collaborative technologies with classroom training.

Internet Technology	Application in Classroom
Email	Handing out reading material, assignments, and other material Submitting completed assignments Making announcements to the whole class Asking questions privately
Discussion group (bulletin board, listserv, or newsgroup)	Announcements to the whole class Asking and answering questions Student lounges where learners can discuss issues among themselves
Chat (instant messaging)	Office hours by the instructor Private conferences between the instructor and learners Study groups or team meetings

Though you want to stick with formats already familiar to participants, you may need to ask them to include just one or two new formats. For example, if authors of classroom courses use Microsoft PowerPoint presentations already, it is reasonable to ask them to learn how to drop Flash animations onto their slides and reasonable to ask learners to obtain the Flash plug-in.

The next step is to select media formats that either work in both the classroom and e-learning realms or that can be converted to a second format that does work in the other realm. For example, Webpages created in HTML work directly in e-learning and can be shown in the classroom. Formats from Microsoft PowerPoint, Word, and some other applications may require conversion. Fortunately, both programs can save content as HTML. With Adobe Acrobat software (www.adobe.com), both PowerPoint and Word can be converted to Acrobat PDF format. Even more conversion options are provided by products and services such as WordToWeb (www.solutionsoft.com) and HTMLTransit (www.systemiksolutions.com) for Microsoft Word and Impatica (www.impatica.com) and Presentia Publisher (www.presedia.com) for PowerPoint.

The third step is to agree on constraints necessary to ensure materials work well in both forms. You may need to limit fonts to those e-learning users are likely to have on their systems. You may need to limit the use of large photographs and other raster graphics to minimize download time. For legibility from the last row of the classroom, you may need to set a minimum size allowed for text. If using the standard "save as HTML" commands built into programs, you may find that intricate layouts or sophisticated animation effects do not survive the conversion, especially if your materials must work for early versions of browsers.

Finally, plan your workflow. Chart the progression of material from authoring through conversion to an alternative format all the way to integration into the finished form. Test to ensure that critical features of the materials are preserved in the process. Test with your most complex materials. And don't forget to put in place controls over who can change the master copies of all materials.

OUR TURN: A CASE STUDY OF BLENDED E-LEARNING

In 1997, William Horton Consulting was asked to help jump-start e-learning in Sweden. The Foundation for Knowledge and Competence Development (Stifelsen För Kunskaps-Och Kompetensutveckling), a consortium of Swedish government, industry, and academia, contracted with us to develop and deliver a Web-based course on designing electronic courses. The goal was to get content providers (university professors) working with industry sponsors and multimedia developers to deploy electronic courses for use throughout Swedish industry. What we created was a learning sandwich.

While discussing the content of this course with our sponsor, we soon realized that few of our potential learners had ever taken any form of WBT, and not many more had been exposed to disk-based training. The bottom line was we needed to introduce our learners to the larger concepts of e-learning. We needed to provide a context for our training and help them get started using Web technology before sending them off to learn the nitty-gritty of actually creating WBT. Furthermore, after taking the training, our learners would need some assistance in applying what they had learned to an actual project. How could we satisfy these requirements? Well, some form of classroom training seemed the perfect solution.

So how did all this become a sandwich? Before beginning the Web-based course, all our learners met in Gothenburg for a two-day seminar. We introduced ourselves, talked about big-picture e-learning issues, and took them on a guided tour of Web-based courses. We set realistic learning goals and helped them develop a strategy for taking the Web-based course over the next six weeks. At the end of the six weeks, we returned for another two-day classroom meeting. Learners were encouraged to discuss their experiences in taking the course—what they liked, what they didn't like—and translate those experiences into guidelines for their own projects.

This blended approach proved very successful and a good use of the available technology. We used the classroom to discuss higher-level ideas and the Web for topics easily learned independently. Almost as important, we all met one another and became comfortable exchanging ideas. This camaraderie helped provide the needed motivation for learners to start and complete this somewhat long and difficult course delivered in a new and challenging medium.

YOUR TURN

For moving your organization to e-learning, a steady guiding hand is more effective than a pounding fist. Consider how you can effectively mix elements of e-learning with proven, conventional techniques.

First, bring the Internet indoors at your organization. In worksheet 7-1, list ways to incorporate Web technology and techniques into your existing classroom training.

Then, discover ways to make sandwiches using your training content. Do you have subjects and learners who would benefit from a learning sandwich that alternates sequences of classroom training and e-learning? Plan ways that you can make sandwiches of e-learning and classroom segments to best effect using figure 7-4.

Worksheet 7-1. Finding ways to bring the Internet into your classroom.

Web or Internet Technology	Possible Application in Your Classroom Training
Web browsing of external sites	
Class Website	
Email	
Internet newsgroups and public discussion groups	
Class discussion group	
Conferencing software (chat, whiteboard, videoconferencing)	
Other:	
Other:	
Other:	

Figure 7-4. Make sandwiches of e-learning and classroom formats.

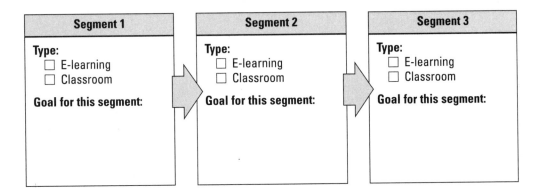

To help your organization make the leap to e-learning, convert your proven classroom materials into electronic formats to distribute via the Web or intranet. To do so, identify suitable material and consider the steps necessary to successfully convert to electronic formats (worksheet 7-2). How can you ensure that recipients can understand the materials out of the context of a classroom?

Worksheet 7-2. Identify ways to convert classroom materials into e-learning formats.

Material	Special Steps for Successful Conversion to E-Learning
Slide presentations	
Graphic and other presentation materials	
Video or audio recordings of presentations	
Validated tests	
Reading materials	
Other:	
Other:	

8

How Can You Develop E-Learning?

Developing original e-learning products is complex, difficult, and expensive. Claims that you can "immediately transform your existing courses to e-learning" deserve the same skepticism as advertisements for miracle stain removers and fad diets.

Developing effective training has never been easy, and e-learning adds more, not fewer, requirements on developers. But e-learning has tremendous potential for reusing content, for guaranteeing consistency, and for ensuring continuous quality improvement heretofore impossible. Consider how developing e-learning is different and what those differences imply for producers and consumers.

Of course, your organization can participate in e-learning without developing its own e-learning courses. You can buy, license, or subscribe to e-learning products developed by others. Or, you can outsource part or all of the development process. See chapter 11 for suggestions on these options. Also, check chapter 10 for information on the people needed to develop e-learning.

This chapter explores each aspect of development and points out what it means in the context of e-learning. First, consider how to get your project started.

How Can You Start Off the Right Way?

You could just dive right into e-learning; however, a little thought and planning at the beginning of the project can lay a firm foundation for all your e-learning efforts. No amount of technology can correct for a hastily conceived and ill-defined project. Many training groups are finding that the move to e-learning offers a chance to rethink their missions and to reconnect with the larger organizations they serve.

Start With Business Objectives

In any form of training, it is usually a good idea to base your training on the business objectives of your organization. E-learning offers a new opportunity to anchor your project to fundamental business and organizational goals. The trick is to write your learning objectives as business goals.

Typical learning objectives specify the knowledge the learner will acquire, for example: "Sales representatives will be able to recall the three primary advantages of each of the organization's latest-generation products." Such an objective specifies what learners will learn but not how it will contribute to the well-being of the organization sponsoring the training.

Here is a business-based training objective: "Over the next 18 months, sales of higher-margin, latest-generation products will double. In addition to training, sales representatives will receive a 15 percent increase in sales commission for these products. Plus, data sheets for these products will be updated. Sales representatives and their managers will attribute 50 percent of the sales increase to the training. Increased profits from sales will pay for the training program three times over." Although more complex, this objective meets the criteria for an effective business-based training objective: It specifies what result will be achieved in enough detail that an objective evaluation is possible. It lists other influencing factors and states limiting assumptions. And, it requires the training to be cost-effective. Such an objective provides a clear charter for development required by e-learning.

Specify Results, Not Methods

Another reason to specify business results is to leave yourself latitude on how to use e-learning to meet those objectives. E-learning is new and evolving rapidly. Your first ideas may not work out, and you may need to shift to plan B or plan C. Be careful not to make your plans so specific that you limit yourself to a particular technology or an exact approach.

Set Realistic Expectations

Your first e-learning project will be the slowest, riskiest, and most expensive one you do. Be careful what you promise. Set realistic expectations among sponsors, builders, subcontractors, and staff. Compared to developing similar classroom training, your first e-learning development project may take four times as long, cost eight times as much, have 10 times as many changes of plan, and be three times as stressful. Tell everyone to buckle his or her seat belt.

Require a commitment from all participants to see the project to the end. Better still, get a commitment to complete multiple projects so you can see where budgets, schedules, and stress levels stabilize.

HOW IS DEVELOPING E-LEARNING DIFFERENT?

How does developing e-learning differ from developing conventional training? Although e-learning may look different and may rely on different technologies, you do not need to scrap your current instructional development methodology. You will, however, need to update it to account for an important aspect of e-learning: E-learning is both learning and software. E-learning thus benefits from three aspects of proven software development methodologies:

- *Rapid prototyping.* E-learning is new. Development requires more experimentation and revision than forms like classroom training, which have evolved over a 500-year span.
- *Modularity.* For pedagogical and economic reasons, most organizations want to design e-learning as a collection of reusable modules rather than one-time performances.
- *Standards.* Reuse of content means that modules from multiple vendors can be combined in a single project. Such integration can only occur upon a basis of technical and pedagogical standards.

Many e-learning developers believe that traditional instructional system design methodology is too slow for modern business training especially in high-technology areas where the business needs for training can change faster than courses can be developed using traditional methods. As a result, these developers frequently rely on a rapid prototyping process.

Most successful development methodologies involve four main phases: analysis, design, building, and evaluating. Rapid prototyping methodologies have these same phases but they are repeated several times in the course of the project. Rather than a straight path, rapid prototyping has more of a corkscrew path because of these iterative cycles (figure 8-1).

First you analyze, then you design, finally you build and evaluate. At first, the prototypes are crude; they are usually little more than pencil sketches on index cards. Toward the end, they approach the final product. But, not everything works as expected, so you must reanalyze, redesign, and rebuild. Such a process is sometimes called the "two steps forward, one step back" approach. Although it might seem inefficient, it is usually the most practical way to deal with the uncertainties of a new form such as e-learning. Because you begin testing designs early, you can quickly identify their shortcomings and correct them before they are too expensive to fix. In the course of a project, this sequence of activities may be repeated several times (figure 8-2).

For e-learning, this development cycle continues throughout the life of the course. Developers continually monitor the effectiveness of the course and make adjustments. New components and content are added. Content is updated and refined. One developer likened this process to changing the tires on a moving

Figure 8-1. Corkscrew path of rapid prototyping for new e-learning forms.

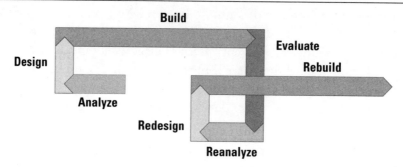

vehicle. Without rapid prototyping, such dynamic, evolving, e-learning products would be impossible.

One of the oft-cited advantages of e-learning is the ability to reuse content in multiple courses and formats. Such an advantage, though, does not come without efforts to design components as reusable modules from the start. Reusable units of training go by several names: learning objects, knowledge objects, reusable content objects. Despite the differences in terminology, the basic idea is the same. A module is a piece that is complete enough that it can be reused in different projects for different purposes.

To design modules, you must first recognize that all levels of e-learning can be designed as modules. A curriculum is made up of course modules. Courses consist of lesson modules, each containing individual topic modules. Each topic may contain multiple content modules (figure 8-3). Table 8-1 describes the content of each level of the modular components.

Figure 8-2. Successive iterations of the analyze-design-build-evaluate cycle.

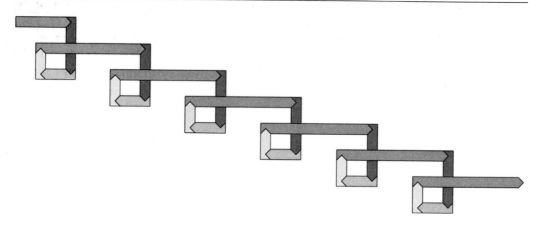

Figure 8-3. Modular design of e-learning.

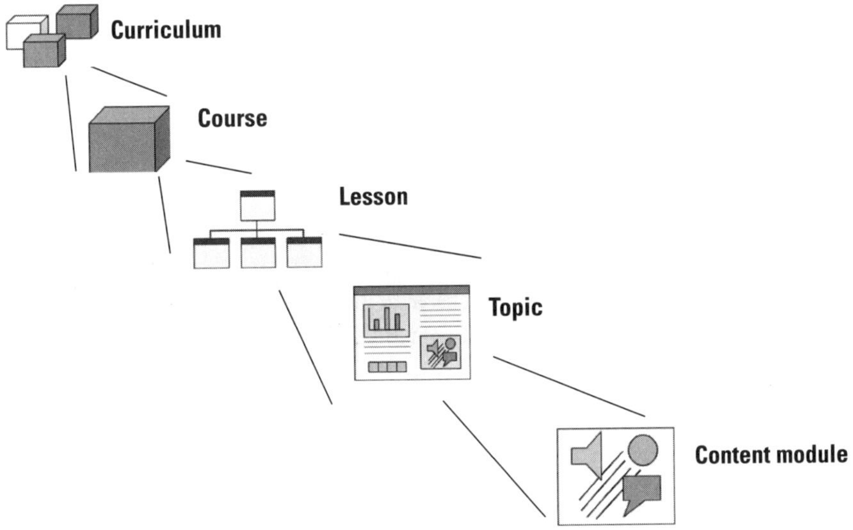

To create reusable modules at each level, design top-down, defining a hierarchy of objectives starting with that for the course (or curriculum if working at that level). The example in figure 8-4 starts with the objective for the overall course. This objective is further elaborated into more specific goals for lessons, which are further decomposed into goals for individual topic modules. Topic modules teach specific beliefs, attitudes, skills, and knowledge.

Table 8-1. Modular components of e-learning.

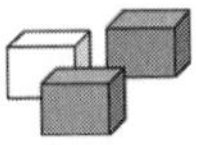	**Curriculum**	A group and sequence of courses; also called a program, collection, or library.
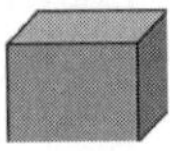	**Course**	A complete unit of study covering a substantial body of knowledge or a complex skill; sometimes called a book.
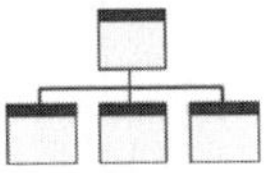	**Lesson**	An organized cluster of related but separate topics; sometimes called a chapter.
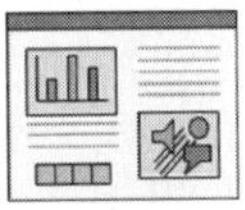	**Topic**	The unit that teaches a single concept; usually includes both a presentation of the concept and an opportunity to practice applying it.
	**Content module**	Media component that contributes to a topic or makes a single point but is not sufficient to stand alone; may consist of sound or video clips, animation sequences, or just paragraphs of text.

Figure 8-4. Hierarchical design of teaching modules for e-learning.

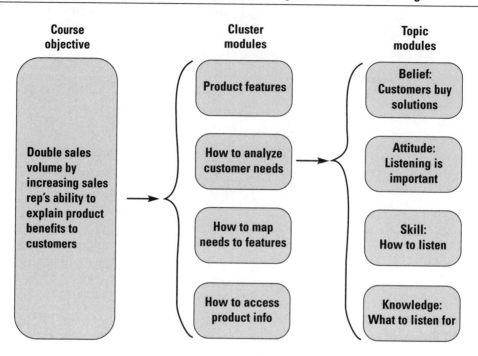

Once you have set the goals for each module, look at how to turn the goal into training. The way to do this is to realize that each module must have a method in addition to the goal (figure 8-5). The method just specifies how the module will meet its goal.

You can specify two types of methods for modules. For higher-level modules, you can specify submodules, that is, a structured sequence of lower-level modules. For example, a lesson module might include a diagram showing the topics included in the lesson and how they are linked together.

For lower-level modules, ones without submodules, spell out the learning experience that will accomplish the goal of the module. Usually you can list the combinations of presentation and practice activities that will completely accomplish the learning goal of the module. In an ideal design, such a modular specification is independent of the technology that will be used to implement the module. And, each such module is completely self-contained. That means that you can include such a module in any learning product that needs to accomplish that module's learning goal.

In a real design, however, take concrete steps to ensure that the resulting module is comprehensible in any of the contexts in which it may eventually appear. Some mortar and caulk may be needed to assemble our building blocks. From the companion Website at www.horton.com/leading/, you can download design forms to help plan learning modules.

Figure 8-5. Typical framework of a learning module.

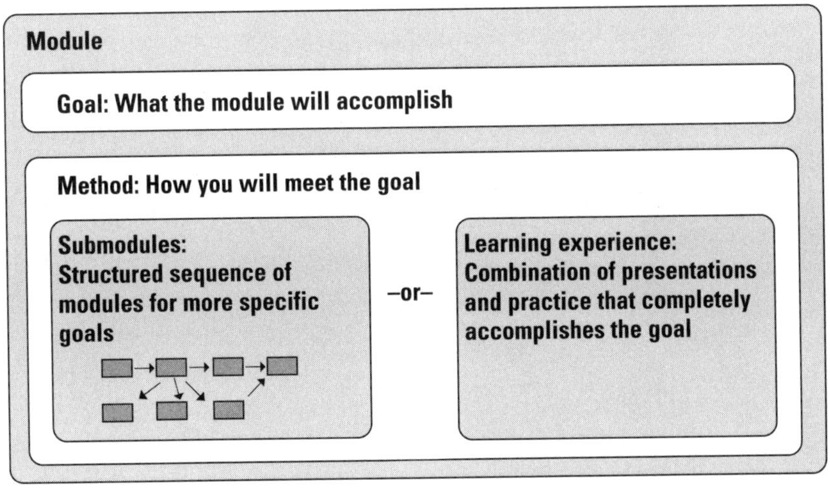

The ultimate goal of reusable modules is interoperability. That means developers can assemble a custom course from modules produced by different vendors using different tools. But modules are reusable only if they are built to a common set of technical and pedagogical standards. The good news is that standards for e-learning are growing as rapidly as e-learning itself. The bad news is that many of these standards are highly technical and only in the early stages of development and adoption. The next section will cover this important topic.

STANDARDS

Should you immediately adopt proposed standards? Should you require compliance in your requests for proposals and purchase orders? Or should you just wait and see how standards evolve? The answers depend primarily on your level of involvement with e-learning development.

If you are developing tools for e-learning or hoping to publish large libraries of courses, you need to identify which standards will affect sales of your products and comply with those standards as they emerge as purchasing forces in the marketplace. If you will be purchasing courses to run under a specific learning management system, you must ensure that both the courses and learning management system can communicate seamlessly and that they follow either public or proprietary standards for data exchange.

If you are just developing courses for your own purposes or will be purchasing courses externally, you have the luxury of waiting until it is clear which standards matter and which are just noble experiments. In any case, you will want to monitor the development of standards and be prepared to adopt them as warranted. The rest of this chapter covers the primary standards efforts for e-learning.

The IEEE Learning Technology Standards Committee

The Learning Technology Standards Committee (LTSC, formerly known as P1484) is a constellation of working groups under the aegis of the Institute of Electrical and Electronics Engineers. The LTSC's mission is to develop technical standards, recommendations, and guidelines for tools, technologies, and design techniques for e-learning.

As of December 2000, the LTSC had 17 working and study groups discussing standards for content packaging, learning management systems, models of learners, definitions of competencies, learning objects, data-interchange protocols, and e-learning terminology. Some of these efforts overlap or subsume standards efforts by Instructional Management Systems (IMS) and others.

For more on the LTSC and its work, see http://grouper.ieee.org/p1484/.

Reasons to Ignore Standards (for Now at Least)

Some in the e-learning community believe it is too early to take standards seriously. They argue that:

- Several standards groups offer overlapping, duplicate, and contradictory standards.
- Many standards are not complete enough to actually endure interoperability.
- Most standards are so technical that they apply only to the programmers of tool suppliers.
- Most standards are written in such academic and technical terms that they are incomprehensible to those who must apply them.
- No clear mechanisms for testing and certifying compliance yet exist.
- Standards will stifle innovation by focusing efforts on compliance rather than on learners' needs.
- Complying with standards adds too much to the costs.
- Standards cover only the less innovative forms of e-learning.
- Standards are overused as marketing ploys aimed at customers who do not realize the limitations of standards.
- Standards are no panacea, and a bit of skepticism can inoculate you against hype.

Advanced Distributed Learning and SCORM

Advanced Distributed Learning (ADL) began as an initiative by the U.S. Department of Defense aimed at improving the quality of training received by U.S. military forces. It has attracted interest from other NATO countries, from defense contractors, and from the training community in general who believe that ADL may have the muscle and discipline to produce effective standards.

The primary focus of ADL is its sharable content object reference model (SCORM) effort, which provides a set of interrelated technical standards for interoperability of learning content. This model incorporates and reconciles emerging standards from the Aviation Industry CBT Committee, IMS, and IEEE LTSC into a single content model. Additionally, SCORM will offer a voluntary testing service and automated tools for testing compliance. It is important to note that passing this testing does not imply certification. Among the primary standards encompassed by SCORM are the following:

■ packaging standard for representing course inventory and organization so courses can run under different learning management systems

■ runtime specifications for how learning management systems can launch courses and modules and how modules can report results back to the learning management system

■ metadata standards for creating and publishing metadata records about courses, lessons, topics, and content modules (based on the IMS metadata standard).

For more on ADL and SCORM, see http://www.adlnet.org/.

Aviation Industry CBT Committee.

The Aviation Industry CBT Committee (AICC) began as a consortium of aviation companies and suppliers concerned with the difficulty of integrating CBT content from the many suppliers on a particular project. As their efforts grew, so did their membership and focus. Today, AICC includes content providers, multimedia producers, and others outside the aviation industry. The AICC has published some of the first guidelines defining how courseware from different suppliers using different tools could be used interchangeably under a learning management system from yet another provider. Though focused initially on disk-based CBT, these guidelines have become the basis for much of the standards work for network-based e-learning solutions.

Furthermore, AICC has published nine AICC guidelines and recommendations (AGR) for interoperability among content and learning management systems. Several of the most important for e-learning are

■ Computer Managed Instruction (AGR006)
■ Courseware Interchange (AGR007)
■ Web-Based Computer Managed Instruction (AGR010).

For more on AICC, see http://www.aicc.org.

IMS Global Learning Consortium

The IMS Global Learning Consortium consists of industry, education, and government organizations working to improve reuse of their content. Although IMS is short for Instructional Management Systems, the organization downplays the full name in favor of the abbreviation. The consortium has produced influential standards on labeling e-learning materials, exchanging administrative data, and packaging materials into courses, including the following:

■ *Metadata tagging.* The IMS learning resources metadata specification prescribes how to make information about courses and other modules available electronically so learners can search for the content they need, for example, from a learning management system. The prescribed method is to publish metadata, which is data about data. For courses, metadata might include the name of the course, its size and length, and the language it uses. The IMS metadata standard has been incorporated into the SCORM initiative.

- *Content packaging.* The IMS content and packaging specification sets forth a format for specifying the content and organization of a course. This format can be used to build a manifest of reusable content objects that make up a course. As such, it provides a course definition independent of any particular learning management system. Microsoft's Learning Resource iNterchange (LRN, pronounced "learn") specification and toolkit are an implementation of this standard (http://www.microsoft.com/elearn/).

- *Test questions.* The IMS question and test specification prescribes a common format for test questions so they can be used in courses and assessments on different systems.

- *Administrative data interchange.* The IMS enterprise information model prescribes how to record and share data about learners, courses, and performance among learning management systems and HR systems. This standard prescribes what to record and how to format it for easy exchange among online systems.

- *Learner information.* The IMS learner information packaging specification lists ways to describe learners so that learning systems can more precisely target the needs of learners.

For more on IMS standards, see www.imsproject.org/specifications.html.

How Are the Standards Efforts Related?

Among the standards groups there is considerable overlap, duplication, competition, and contradiction. But things are not as chaotic as a cursory examination of the Websites of the various groups might indicate. Behind the scenes, there is cooperation and coordination. Figure 8-6 shows how groups involved in e-learning standards are working together.

Most of the proposed standards for e-learning technology come from three of the groups: the Aviation Industry CBT Committee, Advanced Distributed Learning's SCORM effort, and the IMS Global Consortium. Though initially rivals, these groups are now working to coordinate their efforts. Rather than developing competing standards, they tend to adopt the others' standards, add modifications, and send the modifications back to the originating group as a request for changes.

Although these groups are active in developing standards, they lack the mechanism or authority to publish and enforce standards. That's where the IEEE comes in. Its authority as a source of industry standards is recognized and respected. So, after standards are agreed upon by AICC, ADL, and IMS, they are submitted to IEEE to receive its approval.

Figure 8-6. Relationships among standards groups.

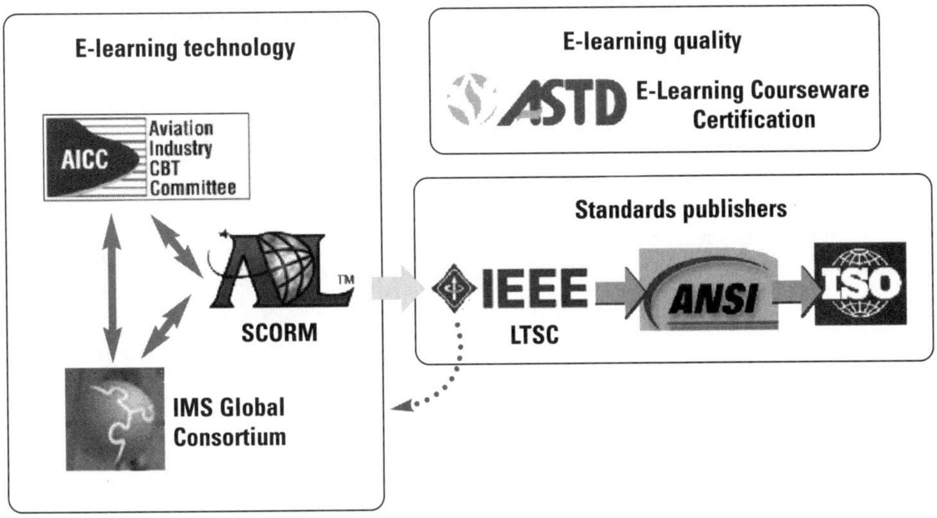

E-learning technology

AICC — Aviation Industry CBT Committee

SCORM

IMS Global Consortium

E-learning quality

ASTD E-Learning Courseware Certification

Standards publishers

IEEE LTSC → ANSI → ISO

The dotted arrow from IEEE back to the technology standards groups indicates that the IEEE Learning Technology Standards committee is also active in originating standards. Its study groups have identified areas where standards are needed and have provided suggestions and feedback to the groups directly developing standards.

Although IEEE standards have great authority, even more authority comes when these standards are published by national international standards agencies. In the United States, standards may be upgraded to national standards by the American National Standards Institute (www.ansi.org) and then by the International Organization for Standardization (ISO, www.iso.ch).

In addition to standards for e-learning technology, their efforts aim to improve the quality effectiveness of the e-learning, regardless of its technological basis. In this area you find ASTD's E-Learning Courseware Certification (eCC). For more on certification, go to www.astd.org/ecertification/.

Understanding the relationships among these standards groups will help you decide which are important to your efforts and which you can safely ignore.

YOUR TURN

How will your organization develop quality e-learning on schedule and within budget? Your first step should be to identify your business objectives. For training projects you have been involved in, identify the underlying business goal that the training supported (worksheet 8-1).

Worksheet 8-1. Identify business goals behind your training projects.

Training Project	Learning Goal	Underlying Business Goal

How can you adapt your instructional systems development process to accommodate the fast pace and rapid evolution of e-learning? Jot down your thoughts in worksheet 8-2.

Worksheet 8-2. How to quicken the pace of instructional development.

Instructional system development process you use:

List some ways to make it faster and more responsive without losing the discipline and quality control it provides:

Would modularity benefit your training? Can you identify specific lessons, topics, and content modules that could be reused in different courses? Try to do so using worksheet 8-3.

Worksheet 8-3. Identify potential learning module components.

Reusable Module Component	Where Can You Use It?

Visit the Websites for the various standards groups. Do any of them seem to apply to what you are doing (worksheet 8-4)? Or, should you wait until standards are built into the tools you use and the components you purchase?

Worksheet 8-4. Select applicable standards for your e-learning efforts.		
Standards Group	**Possible Application to Your E-Learning Courses? (✓)**	**How to Incorporate Standards Into Your Work?**
IEEE Learning Technology Standards Committee http://grouper.ieee.org/p1484/		
Advanced Distributed Learning and SCORM www.adlnet.org/		
Aviation Industry CBT Committee www.aicc.org		
IMS Global Learning Consortium www.imsproject.org		
ASTD Courseware Certification www.astd.org/ecertification/		

9

What Tools and Technology Will You Need?

Computer hardware, telecommunications links, and computer software are required for producers to author courses, for hosts to conduct and administer them, and for consumers to access and display them. Figure 9-1 shows the primary hardware, network connections, and software required for each of these activities. The rest of this chapter surveys the technologies needed for an e-learning application. If you do not want to make technology a focus of your efforts, see chapter 11 for suggestions on how others can provide the technologies you need.

Keep in mind that sometimes you cannot control what technology the learner has. It is best to start with what learners already have and work backwards to ensure that you are not creating materials that they can't access and display effectively.

Figure 9-1. Technologies needed for creating and accessing e-learning courses.

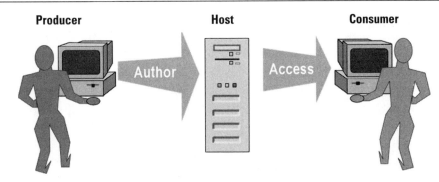

Producer	Host	Consumer
• Multimedia workstation	• Network server	• Personal computer
• Moderate-speed connection	• High-speed connection	• Moderate-speed connection
• Authoring software	• Web server software	• Browser and media players

COMPUTER HARDWARE FOR E-LEARNING

Computers are needed to author, host, and access e-learning. Let's look at the requirements for each activity. Design forms to help you specify your hardware requirements are available from this book's companion Website at www .horton.com/leading/.

For the Learner to Access E-Learning

On what type of computer will learners take your e-learning? If you control what computer learners use, you can design the e-learning course first and then specify the computer hardware necessary to access and take it. This might be the case if e-learning is taken at a special e-learning center where you provide the computers. It may also be the case where your internal IT department can prescribe certain minimum standards.

More commonly, though, designers of e-learning must accommodate the computer hardware learners already own. Before making any technology decisions, survey your learners to gauge the capabilities of their computers with regard to

■ screen size (in pixels)
■ number of colors they can display
■ sound playback
■ amount of memory (RAM), especially if multimedia will be used
■ processor speed and type (for example, 850-MHz Pentium III processor).

In gathering this information, make sure you clearly identify where and when learners will take e-learning. Will they take it from their desktop computer at work, from a laptop computer on the road, or from a home computer on weekends and evenings?

For Hosting E-Learning

Hosting e-learning requires a Web server. Such servers are essentially high-performance PCs designed to dispatch Webpages and other media in response to requests from users. Such machines need fast processors, big disks, and lots of memory. Many models come with redundant power supplies, mirrored disks, and hot-swappable disks to minimize downtime. If your courses incorporate extensive audio and video, or if you use real-time collaborative tools for conferencing and screen-sharing, you may require separate servers optimized for these special needs.

Precise recommendations are not easy, so consult with your hardware supplier or IT department staff. They will need to know how many courses you will host, how large your files will be, how many learners you expect, and what file formats you will use.

For the Producer to Author E-Learning

The producers of e-learning must prepare, capture, and assemble the various media for the e-learning course. They typically require a powerful workstation capable of running several programs simultaneously. This means the workstation will need copious memory, a large hard disk, and a spacious screen. Although specifications and prices would be out of date by the time the ink of this book dries, as a general rule, plan to spend twice as much on the author's workstation as on the computer that a learner will use to take the resulting course.

If the course will include multimedia, you may need to budget for a digital videocamera, microphones, music keyboard, scanner, and other devices for capturing the media you will include as well.

Authors also require a computer setup to simulate the one on which learners take e-learning. It is easy for course authors, working on large-screen, multimedia workstations, to soar beyond the capabilities of the three-year-old laptop computers their learners possess.

> ### Bits, Bytes, and Ks
>
> To understand telecommunications speed ratings, you need to learn a bit of technospeak. It's really simple provided you keep a few definitions in mind. Quantities of data are usually stated in multiples of bits and bytes. A bit is a single binary digit: on or off, yes or no, 1 or 0. A byte is 8 bits and can be thought of as the amount used to store a single character from the Roman alphabet. Chinese, Japanese, and other languages with thousands of characters require two bytes per character.
>
> For a computer, a bit or even a byte is not very much; so we often talk in larger units. A kilobyte is 1,024 bytes and is abbreviated simply as K. Yes, a kilometer is 1,000 meters, but a kilobyte is 1,024 bytes. It's a computer thing. A megabyte (MB) is likewise a bit more than a million bytes and a gigabyte (GB) is something more than a thousand million bytes. Another abbreviation you may run into is Kb, which stands for kilobit, not to be confused with K or sometimes KB, which stands for kilobyte.
>
> When we discuss the speed of a communications link, we specify how much data it can transmit per second. For example, we might say that a modem transmits 56.6 Kbps (kilobits per second). A higher speed link may be rated in megabits per second or Mbps.
>
> If you keep in mind the distinction between bit and byte, you will not make the common mistake of forgetting to multiply or divide by eight when converting file sizes in K (kilobytes) to communications speeds in Kbps (kilobits per second).

NETWORK CONNECTIONS FOR E-LEARNING

All participants need a network connection. Learners need to access the hosting server to take the course. Additionally, producers need to be able to access the host to upload course materials.

For the Learner to Access E-Learning

A learner's network connection should be as fast as possible. Pages appear quicker, sounds play smoother, and the video does not stutter. If you don't have control over the speed of the learner's connection, it is essential to know what that speed is and design for it. A course designed for a 1-Mbps T1 line will seem awkward on a 128-Kbps ISDN line and impossibly frustrating on a 56.6-Kbps telephone modem.

Remember that the connection speed depends on where the learner plugs in. The learner may have a fast connection at work, a moderate-speed connection at home, a slow one at the cheap hotel room, and a really slow one when connecting using a wireless modem. Make sure you know where and when people will take your course.

Suppose your goal is for each page to download within 10 seconds, even when learners access the course over a 56.6-Kbps modem. You can do the math then. Because actual communication speeds over a noisy telephone line may be half the modem's rated speed, use an effective rate of 30 Kbps. In 10 seconds, that link can carry 300 Kb of information. Dividing by 8 bits per byte, we arrive at a page size limit of 37.5 K.

For Hosting E-Learning

For the server, only one speed will do: fast. To calculate the speed required, multiply the number of simultaneous users by the average page size, including graphics and any multimedia. Perhaps at peak times you expect to have 10,000 learners, each of whom accesses a 250-K page every 30 seconds. You will need at least:

$$10,000 \text{ learners} \times 250 \text{ K} \times 8 \text{ (bits per byte)} \div 30 \text{ seconds}$$
$$= 667 \text{ Kbps connection speed}$$

In this case, to be on the safe side and to allow for growth, you'd probably want to specify a 1-Mbps (1,024-Kbps) connection.

For the Producer to Upload and Test E-Learning

The author of e-learning will need a network connection to upload materials to the host. The author will also need to test the materials from the server. At a minimum, the producer will need a connection of the same speed as that used by learners. That way the author observes the same bottlenecks and awkward pauses as learners—and is motivated to fix them before learners access the course.

If the author is spending considerable time uploading to the server, you may want a second high-speed connection for convenience. Always remember to test on a connection of the same speed as the one used by learners.

Testing communications speed at 2 a.m. with a single user accessing a single text page is hardly a realistic measurement. Test with realistic numbers of learners accessing realistic numbers of pages at realistic times from realistic locations.

SOFTWARE FOR E-LEARNING

Picking software for e-learning is fortunately very complex: Complex because there are so many factors you must consider and fortunate because we have so many good products from which to choose.

When you begin writing your technology plan you will encounter several overlapping, fuzzily defined categories of software for use in creating the various levels of e-learning components. Your choice is further complicated by the need for maintaining compatibility among the software programs for authoring, hosting, and delivering courses. This book can't solve all this complexity, but it will provide a framework for making decisions.

For the Learner to Access E-Learning

Learners require a Web browser and some media players to take e-learning. The media players display media that cannot be displayed by the Web browser itself. Web browsers display text and graphics. The text must be encoded following the rules of HTML, and the graphics must be of a format that the particular browser can display. Other media are displayed through the use of separate media players. Microsoft Internet Explorer (IE) and Netscape Navigator browsers offer roughly equivalent features, though some significant differences do exist and new versions are released frequently.

> ### Myth of the Fast Network
>
> You have probably heard lines like these: "We're going to put our e-learning on the company intranet, and it's fast" and "All of our customers have fast Internet connections in their offices." Before you design with a fast network in mind, take a moment for a reality check. You do not need a fast network if any of the following are true:
> - Many of your learners take courses from home or a hotel using a dial-up connection and a slow modem.
> - Your course uses so much video or other heavy media that even a fast network seems slow.
> - Materials have to pass through many gateways, routers, proxy servers, and firewalls to get to learners.
> - So many learners access the course simultaneously that server overload, not network speed, is the bottleneck.
> - Your company keeps adding more and more users to the network.

The learner's choice of browser is closely linked to their choice of operating system. Learners on Microsoft's Windows operating system are likely to have a comparable version of the IE browser installed. The IE browser is also available for Macintosh computers. Netscape browsers are available for Windows, Macintosh, Linux, and some other Unix systems.

If all your learners are on Windows systems, you may want to target the IE browser to take advantage of some of its specific features. If your learners are on various operating systems, then you will need to target the Netscape browser. A third choice is to target and support only a common subset of features supported by both browsers. To offer the highest performance, some designers try to target a specific version of a particular browser. Others, aiming for a broader market, restrict themselves to the features provided by earlier versions of both browsers.

Media players extend the capability of the browser to display media and interact with the learner. Media players that display within the context of the browser are typically called plug-ins or controls. If they appear as separate programs, they are usually referred to as players or viewers.

Some players are used to display sound, animation, and video. Some plug-ins are required to display e-learning developed in proprietary formats such as that for Macromedia Authorware or Mentergy Quest courseware. Others are used to interact with the user, for example to play a game or conduct a chat session.

Several e-learning projects have failed because they required technically unsophisticated learners to download and install too many separate media players. In writing your technology plan, consider which media players learners already have installed on their systems and how you can minimize the number of additional ones you require.

For Hosting E-Learning

Making e-learning available over a network requires, at a minimum, a generic Web server. It may also require systems to manage and administer courses and curricula, to allow learners to collaborate, and to serve audio and video clips.

Web Server. The core Web server software package consists of a bundle of capabilities, most basic of which is the ability to respond to requests for HTML pages. Most Web servers include email and newsgroup services as well. Two popular packages are the Apache Web server (www.apache.org), which runs on Windows, Linux, and some other Unix operating systems, and Microsoft's Internet Information Server (www.microsoft.com/servers/), which comes with Windows 2000 Server and NT Server operating systems. Keep in mind that your choice of Web server will limit your choices of what other software can run on your server. Pick a coordinated package.

Learning Management Systems. These systems manage the process of instruction primarily at the curriculum level. They provide tools to define, sequence, and offer courses and modules. They simplify administrative tasks such as enrolling learners, maintaining rosters, and scheduling training events. They can track the performance of learners, recording their access of course components and their scores on assessments. Learning management systems can also generate detailed reports summarizing each learner's progress.

Some learning management systems include components to help track financial data and conduct e-commerce. Such components can validate purchase orders, bill internal departments, and accept payments. Others include elements of knowledge management. They provide tools to analyze competencies, calculate skill gaps, and link such measurements to HR management systems.

Learning management systems range from simple to complex. Upper-end systems can cost up to $250,000 and require months of custom programming and consulting services to implement. Lower-end systems have only basic capabilities, cost a few thousand dollars, and can be implemented in a few days by server administrators.

Some popular learning management packages include the Docent (www.docent.com), Pathlore (www.pathlore.com), Saba (www.saba.com), Learnframe.com, Click2Learn Librarian (www.click2learn.com), and Mentergy's Manager's Edge (www.mentergy.com) systems.

Some products integrate learning management features with tools for authoring courses and building collaboration among instructors and students. These more comprehensive products are sometimes called learning environments, virtual campuses, or virtual training centers. They include products like WebCT (www.webct.com) and TopClass (www.wbtsystems.com) systems.

Collaboration Software. This software component makes possible real-time events, such as class meetings, chat sessions, instant messaging, videoconferences, and other capabilities beyond the basic collaboration tools provided in the Web server or learning management system. Popular among producers are the Centra Symposium (www.centra.com), InterWise Millennium (www.inter wise.com), and Microsoft NetMeeting and Exchange Server (www.micro soft.com) collaboration servers. The LearnLinc Virtual Campus and Virtual Classroom (www.mentergy.com) and LearningSpace (www.lotus.com) tools, combine collaboration mechanisms with learning management features.

If your needs for collaboration hosting are limited, you may be able to lease or borrow time on someone else's server. Perhaps your e-learning efforts can use the same collaboration server used for business meetings in your organization. Or, you may want to use MShow (www.mshow.com), PlaceWare (www.place ware.com), or other Web-based collaboration services.

Media Servers. Media servers are software tools optimized for delivering particular media and file formats. Their goal is to smoothly and efficiently distribute digital media, such as sound or video that could bog down an ordinary Web server. These servers include the RealSystem server from RealNetworks.com and Microsoft's Windows Media Services (www.microsoft.com), part of the Windows 2000 server. Before choosing a media server, be sure you know which file formats you will be delivering because these servers do not support the exact same types of media. Consider a media server, perhaps on a separate machine, if you are using large amounts of audio or video or if you will be broadcasting live presentations.

For the Producer Authoring E-Learning

Producing an e-learning project can require using several different computer programs to create hundreds of computer files in several different file formats. Let's look at the tools to add to your shopping list.

Course-Authoring Programs. For assembling your course, you may want to use a tool that can manage and integrate the separate pieces of the course. For such a tool, you may have to combine separate products, such as Macromedia's Dreamweaver and CourseBuilder Extension programs (www.macromedia.com) or Mentergy's Designer's Edge and Net Synergy program (www.mentergy.com).

Or, you may want to use one of the tools originally designed for disk-based CBT, such as ToolBook II by Click2Learn (www.click2learn.com) or Authorware by Macromedia (www.macromedia.com). Such CBT tools produce courses in a proprietary file format and require special viewer software for distribution over the Web. However, they may be just the ticket if you already have a large investment in ToolBook or Authorware courseware that you now want to make available over the Web.

A third possibility is one of the server-based tools like the WebCT or TopClass programs, which incorporate learning management features as well.

Webpage Authoring Programs. An efficient Webpage editor is another essential. Some opt for a WYSIWYG ("what you see is what you get") page editor such as Macromedia Dreamweaver (www.macromedia.com), Microsoft FrontPage (www.microsoft.com), or Adobe GoLive (www.adobe.com). Others prefer to edit the page code directly, especially when writing JavaScript or fine-tuning advanced features. They may prefer the HomeSite tool (www .allaire.com) or just a NotePad or SimpleText editor.

Media Authoring Programs. Media editing programs create and refine the various graphics, animations, sounds, video clips, and other media you will include in your course. Good news! Most media editing programs can now save their creations in formats usable in e-learning. In this category you may want to include programs to convert existing materials to a Web-ready format. Most word processors, spreadsheets, and other programs can save their output as HTML or GIF files for use on the Web. For other computer applications, conversion programs such as the Adobe Acrobat (www.adobe.com) publishing software can help.

Representative Toolkits. Consider a couple of diagrams from some technology plans for several e-learning projects (figures 9-2 and 9-3). Each diagram shows the combination of tools chosen for each activity (authoring, hosting, delivery)

Figure 9-2. Example technology plan for a self-paced WBT training course.

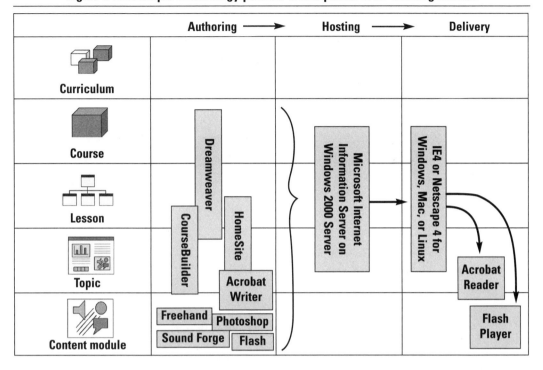

and for each level of e-learning product (curriculum, course, lesson, topic, content module). Though fairly typical, these toolkits are in no way recommendations. Your situation is certain to be different.

A self-paced WBT training course, as depicted in figure 9-2, can have relatively simple tool requirements, especially if it limits its use of media. In this case the author assembled the course in Dreamweaver (www.macromedia.com), using the CourseBuilder Extension components for tests and other interactions. For fine-tuning the HTML code, the author sometimes edited individual pages in the HomeSite HTML editor (www.macromedia.com).

Because the course had extensive reading materials, it was decided to provide those materials in Adobe Acrobat format so that learners could print precisely formatted copies as necessary. All that was required to do this was to print the document from the word processor using the Acrobat PDF Writer (www.adobe.com) print driver.

Illustrations were drawn in Macromedia FreeHand (www.macromedia .com) and polished and compressed using the Adobe Photoshop program (www.adobe.com). A few animations were created using the Macromedia Flash program. Illustrations for these animations were created in Macromedia FreeHand, and sounds for these animations were recorded and edited using the SoundForge editor (www.sonicfoundry.com).

All of the resulting Webpages, graphics, sounds, and animations were uploaded to the Web server running Windows 2000 server. No other server software was required in this case.

Learners took the course using whatever browser they already had. They did, however, need the Adobe Acrobat Reader (www.adobe.com) and Flash Player plug-ins (www.macromedia.com) to view the corresponding media. The learners were able to download these programs from the Web.

The plan for a virtual university (figure 9-3) is a bit more complex because it involves many students taking multiple courses, some of which contain live class meetings. Managing the whole curriculum was a WebCT (www .webct.com) learning management system on an Apache Web server (www.apache.org). The individual Webpages for the course were created in HomeSite (www.allaire.com) and inserted into the WebCT database.

Several programs were used to create and deliver media. Illustrations were prepared using the Adobe Illustrator and Photoshop programs (www.adobe .com), animations in the Macromedia Flash editor (www.macromedia.com), sounds in the SoundForge editor (www.sonicfoundry.com), and video sequences in Adobe Premier (www.adobe.com). The illustrations and animations were stored directly on the Web server, but the sound and video files were saved in the RealAudio and RealVideo formats and uploaded to a separate RealSystem

Figure 9-3. Example technology plan for a virtual university.

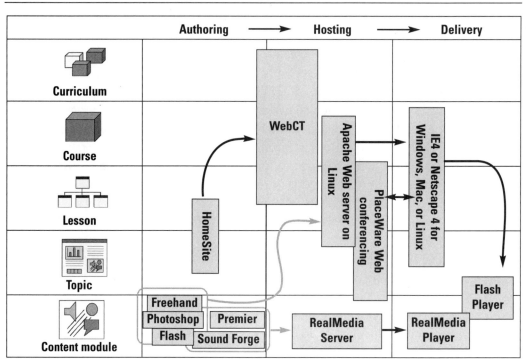

server (www.realnetworks.com). For collaboration, the virtual university used PlaceWare's Conference Center (www.placeware.com) conferencing software running on the local server.

Learners used a variety of browsers. Animations were displayed by the Flash player (www.macromedia.com) and sounds and video by the RealMedia player (www.real.com). Connections to the conferencing center were through the Web browser.

How Do You Pick the Tools?

There is no surefire way to pick tools. Keep in mind that some products meet multiple requirements, but some capabilities may require multiple products. You may even have to assemble your own tools to achieve some capabilities. Some capabilities may not even be possible yet. As you select tools, mistakes are inevitable, but there are steps you can take to put the odds in your favor:

- Design first, then buy.
- First, design your ideal course, and then buy the tools needed to implement it.
- Design a few courses (on paper at least), and decide how you want to deliver these courses over the next few years.
- List the capabilities such courses will require.
- Map these capabilities to products that provide these capabilities.

Try Before You Buy

Before you commit to a product, try to learn what using it will be like. Try out a demonstration copy of the product with a representative sample of your materials. Mine the supplier's Website for detailed information about the product. If possible, test the product support by calling in a problem or two. Examine copies of training materials for course authors and administrators. Finally, check the product's support forums or newsgroups for complaints and kudos. Ask yourself these questions:

- Does the product provide the features I need most?
- Does the product integrate well with related products from other suppliers?
- How mature is the product?
- Is the product reliable and efficient?
- Does the product comply with industry standards and does it use common file formats?
- How quickly and easily can you enter your material into the product? And how quickly and easily can you get it out?

- If viewers or players are needed, are they free? Are they easy to download and install?
- Can you easily extend and customize the product to meet your exact needs?

Look Beyond the Software's Capabilities

Never buy a product from the bullet list of its features alone. Consider other factors that will affect the total cost and effectiveness of the tool or technology:

- *The needs and capabilities of learners.* What features do learners need? How much can they handle?
- *Constraints imposed by the tool or technology.* What kinds of e-learning can they create?
- *Financial condition and longevity of the supplier.* Will the company be around to fix bugs and make enhancements?
- *Independent support services available.* Are there consultants and contractors, newsgroups and forums, and third-party books and training to help you with your development effort?

Your Turn

What tools and technologies will be required for your e-learning projects? (Various design forms are available from this book's companion Website at www.horton.com/leading/ to guide you in specifying the technologies required for your project.)

Using worksheet 9-1, list the hardware, network connections, and software that will be required by producers, hosts, and consumers of your e-learning.

Worksheet 9-1. Make your technology shopping list.			
	Producer	**Host**	**Consumer**
Hardware			
Network Connection	Speed:____Kbps	Speed:____Kbps	Speed:____Kbps
Software			
For each item on your list, check off the ones already in place.			

On worksheet 9-2, list the specific software tools required for each level and function. Show specific relationships among tools, for example which tool prepares content integrated by other tools.

List questions in worksheet 9-3 that you can use to screen products and suppliers. Think of questions that will help you identify products and organizations you will be comfortable working with in the coming years.

Worksheet 9-2. Elaborate on your software plan.			
	Authoring	**Hosting**	**Delivery**
Curriculum			
Course			
Lesson			
Topic			
Content Module			

Worksheet 9-3. List questions for suppliers.	
Product Group or Supplier	**Questions**

10

Whom Should You Have on Your E-Learning Team?

With all the focus on technology, it is easy to forget the most important part of any e-learning project: people. If the right people make the right decisions at the right time, their organization can realize the full potential of e-learning.

ASSEMBLE A MULTITALENTED TEAM

Moving an organization to e-learning is a complex, sprawling, dynamic endeavor. It requires a range of skills, talents, knowledge, and viewpoints. The best way to meet this requirement is with a dynamic, multitalented team (figure 10-1).

Figure 10-1. Assemble a talented, dynamic team for your e-learning projects.

A team is not a herd. Although the total range of abilities required for e-learning is large, the number of people actually involved is still manageable because some individuals can perform multiple roles, some activities can be outsourced (see chapter 11), and not everyone is needed on every phase of the effort.

Team membership is dynamic. At each milestone in the project, you may need to adjust team membership to better accomplish the next phase of work. The actual makeup of the team at any point in the project will depend on several factors, such as

- size and scope of the project
- amount of work outsourced
- number of multitalented participants you can recruit
- specific media and technologies required.

For example, during early analysis work, designers actively involve learners to determine their needs. Later, during phases when course material is under development, multimedia developers may be the most active team members.

The rest of this chapter inventories the specific talents, skills, and knowledge required. Though it does so under headings corresponding to job roles, these roles are broadly defined and need not match actual job titles. Some people will be able to perform several roles, especially on a small- or medium-sized project. Also remember that you can outsource tasks your organization does not want to perform itself (see chapter 11).

To Manage the Project

Managing e-learning projects is rather like managing any complex, creative endeavor. The manager of e-learning can be compared to an old-style Hollywood producer overseeing creative talents, managing complex projects, and ensuring financial returns.

E-learning requires recruiting, supervising, and motivating creative, energetic, independent-thinking, and sometimes strong-willed specialists in a way that focuses their efforts on the common goal. Furthermore, the manager must do so without a deep knowledge of all the esoteric disciplines involved.

Management of e-learning also requires scheduling, budgeting, and tracking the various tasks and resources of the project.

> ### One Person or Many?
>
> As you look at the job roles listed in the text and in table 10-1, you may notice that some of the names are singular (lead designer, course integrator, project leader), and some are plural (multimedia developers, programmers, module designers). If a name is singular, that indicates that there should be only one person in this role—even on a large project. If the name is plural, that means a project may have one person or several people in that role, depending on the size and complexity of the project.

The ideal project manager is well organized and able to coordinate hundreds or thousands of details without losing sight of the overall goal.

To Design the Course

Designing instructionally and financially sound courses requires analyzing the needs for learning and specifying detailed solutions. It does not include actually constructing and integrating the content, which is part of the build stage described later.

Lead Designer. Although aspects of course design can be delegated, most successful e-learning development projects require a strong lead designer. The lead designer may delegate design of portions of the course to module designers and may be assisted by specialists and consultants, but it is the lead designer who is responsible for consistently executing a sound instructional strategy.

The primary skill of the lead designer is instructional design or pedagogy. The designer must understand instructional strategies and tactics for teaching a specific subject to a specific learner. Because e-learning courses are software, the designer must know software architecture principles, especially those relating to designing reusable modules and performing rapid prototyping.

Likewise, an understanding of effective user-interface design, especially for Web-based applications, is critical to e-learning design. The designer should know how to lay out a screen, implement navigation conventions, and conduct usability testing.

Finally, the designer must fully understand the needs of the consumers of training because no business endeavor can succeed without carefully targeting its market.

The lead designer defines the strategy and overall design specifications for the project. Keeping the learning objectives of the project in mind, the lead designer works with technical specialists to select appropriate technology on which to build the course. The lead designer sets forth a strategy for creating reusable components and spells out the development methodology the project will follow. The lead designer specifies layouts, color schemes, typography, and other aspects of design that apply throughout the project and sees that these decisions are incorporated into templates that will be used to create content.

Module Designers. On large, complex projects, the lead designer may need to delegate design of specific lessons and topics to other designers. These second-tier designers work with the lead designer to articulate the objectives for the components they are designing. Module designers then translate objectives into plans and specifications for the modules necessary to carry out these objectives. Module designers must work under the framework set forth by the lead designer. They must follow overall project standards and use prescribed templates. Though module designers do not need the big-picture view or breadth of experience possessed by the lead designer, they should have strong instructional design skills and must understand the business purposes of the overall project.

Subject Matter Experts. Designers must have ready access to subject matter experts, though these experts need not be active members of the design team. If the e-learning project covers the same subjects as existing classroom courses do, instructors for those courses can provide subject knowledge.

To Build Content

Builders fulfill the design using tools and technologies specified by the lead designer. Building e-learning can require a range of specialists in media and technology to write the material, create graphics, integrate multimedia, write programming, and assemble the modules and topics into a course.

Course Integrator. Building a complex e-leaning product can require assembling hundreds or thousands of separate HTML pages, JavaScript libraries, GIF and JPEG images, Flash animations, Java applets, video sequences, and other content. It can also require adding special code to make the course run effectively under a learning management system, linking to discussion forums and chat rooms and incorporating e-commerce components to let learners pay by credit card. Getting all these pieces working together is the role of the course integrator.

The course integrator may have to set up the course framework of menus, course map log-in screens, links to reference materials, and so on before actually importing the lessons and all their content. Additionally, the course integrator may be responsible for quality assurance testing to make sure links go where they should, content displays correctly, and student data is tracked accurately.

Writer. Even in an era of television and multimedia, words are still the primary conveyor of knowledge, especially on e-learning projects that must cover conceptual subjects or deliver content over low-bandwidth connections. No doubt about it: E-learning requires strong writing skills. It requires someone who can write for display and for voice and who can understand how these forms differ from each other and how they differ from writing for print media. Because screen space is limited, the writing must be succinct. And, because learners should not be expected to decipher cryptic prose, writing must be clear and direct even when explaining difficult concepts. To keep learners reading or listening, the style should be lively and interesting.

Engage the services of a professional copyeditor. A fresh pair of eyes can catch typographic errors and pick up redundancies and omissions. Every word that is pruned will help improve the visual spacing on a Webpage and help the information load more quickly on the learners' computers. A copyeditor can also polish the contributions of subject matter experts and others on your team for whom English is a second language.

Graphics Specialists. In e-learning, graphics may be as important as words, especially for teaching complex subjects to learners with limited language skills. E-learning requires not only subject-specific illustrations, but also banners, navigation buttons, and icons.

The visual designer you employ should be able to craft simple, functional, attractive graphics that communicate clearly and download quickly. The designer must combine strong drawing skills with an understanding of file formats, color palettes, and compression algorithms for digital graphics.

Multimedia Developers. If your e-learning uses more than simple text and graphics to convey information, you will need multimedia developers. Depending on which media you use, you may need videographers, computer animators, sound recording technicians, and musicians.

When interviewing these specialists, consider their media skills. Just as knowing how to type does not make one a great writer, knowing how to use a multimedia authoring tool does not make one an effective multimedia author. Examine the multimedia specialist's portfolio to ensure that it matches the tone and style of presentation needed for your subject and your learners. Make sure that the specialist understands the difference between multimedia for sales and marketing and that for e-learning. And, ensure that the specialist can work within your constraints of screen size and network connection speed while producing the required file formats.

The need for many specialists can certainly bust all but the largest budgets. Do not panic. If your needs for multimedia are modest, you can often double up the work. Many illustrators can handle light animation, and most videographers can record and edit sound. HTML coders may be able to write some JavaScripts, and most programmers can handle some HTML coding on the side.

HTML/XML Coders. On a simple project, no one may ever need to directly create or edit HTML or XML code. Sophisticated projects, however, may require tailored HTML templates for pages and content modules. These templates can then be used in the authoring program by content creators to ensure consistency. Advanced projects may require creating style sheets to precisely control page formatting or writing XML document type definitions to enforce the organization of content. The advanced features of Dynamic HTML may be used to create visual transitions and simple animations. These activities require a deep knowledge of the specified formats.

In addition to coding HTML and XML, the coder may take on some light-duty programming tasks, such as writing simple JavaScripts to add interactivity and error checking to Webpages.

Programmers. Good e-learning can be created with no programming by developers. However, if you plan to create highly interactive and original e-learning, some programming may be required. Programming requires general software development skills, knowledge of a particular programming language, and, perhaps, the ability to operate a specific software development environment.

Before hiring a programmer, you need to define your programming needs. A Java programmer accustomed to Sun Microsystem's Java 2 development environment may be ill equipped to write ActionScript programs using Macromedia's Flash animator and vice versa.

Among the main types of programming that may be part of advanced e-learning products are browser scripting, server scripting, content scripting, and other advanced programming. Browsers can run programs written in scripting languages they understand. Netscape and IE browsers can run programs written in JavaScript. Microsoft's IE browser can also run programs written in Visual Basic Scripting Edition. Such scripting languages are relatively easy to learn. They are most often used to add interactivity to Webpages.

Likewise, servers can run programs or scripts. Two popular server-scripting technologies are Active Server Pages and Java Server Pages. Server scripts can be used to add interactivity to Webpages, track data, and connect to databases.

Several media authoring tools allow developers to incorporate programming directly into multimedia content modules. For example, Macromedia's Flash animator incorporates its ActionScript language to let developers create highly interactive and adaptive animations.

Even more sophisticated programming may be required for creating Java applets or servlets or ActiveX controls. However, such programming efforts border on pure software development and are not likely to be a big part of a content creation effort.

To Provide the Technical Infrastructure

Before e-learning can begin, someone must link the computers of developers, course hosts, and learners together to make the technology available and usable by all concerned.

Network/Server Administrators. Someone must string the wires, plug in the routers and gateways, bolt on the firewalls, and get the whole network up and running. Typically, this work is done by the IT departments of the organizations offering and taking the e-learning.

Servers are required to host the course, stream media, and enable collaboration among learners. A server administrator will be required to set up the basic server hardware and software, install and configure additional software, and perform backups and other routine maintenance. The IT department typically does such chores; however, some training departments take on these chores for greater control and security.

Server/Database Programmers. To track learners, record student actions, maintain online discussions, and share data with HR systems, e-learning systems may include their own databases or connect to existing corporate databases. These efforts may require installing and configuring the databases as well as some custom programming to transfer data to and from them.

Technical Support Specialists. Infrastructure is more than wires and computers. An often-overlooked part of the technical infrastructure for e-learning is the advice and support required by users. Many early e-learning projects have failed because learners could not master the basic technologies required for e-learning.

Both consumers and producers of e-learning may require assistance setting up workstations, connecting to the network, installing plug-ins and other software, and overcoming technical glitches. Those providing technical support must combine equal amounts of technical knowledge and human empathy. Before rolling out e-learning, decide who will provide such support and make sure it is just a mouse click or phone call away.

To Conduct E-Learning

Once the course is developed and the technical infrastructure is in place, you still must conduct the training. Even self-directed e-learning will require some human support.

Curriculum Administrator. Someone, typically called an e-learning administrator, oversees operations of the e-learning curriculum available to an organization. The administrator is responsible for announcing courses, registering learners, collecting fees, and answering enrollment questions.

Course Facilitator. Many e-learning courses have an assigned facilitator. The facilitator is not the same as an instructor in classroom training. The facilitator typically assists learners but does not actively direct or lead them. The facilitator answers questions about the course, solves problems as they arise, moderates online discussions and chat sessions, and attempts to motivate lagging learners.

The facilitator must have adequate knowledge of the subject matter and of e-learning technologies. If communicating with learners through email or online discussions, the facilitator must be able to express both factual information and emotional concern in writing.

The facilitator must have the right interpersonal skills, too. A good facilitator is helpful without having to lead or control. And, the facilitator must possess great reserves of patience and sympathy for confused and frustrated e-learners who seem to make the same mistakes and ask the same silly questions over and over again.

Online Instructor. Web-conducted classroom courses are led by an online instructor, who, like the instructor in the classroom, prepares and presents material, demonstrates skills, answers questions, and leads discussions. The online instructor must carry out these responsibilities using videoconferencing, chat, discussion forums, email, and other Internet and digital technologies that are available for communicating with unseen, distant learners. The online instructor requires both technical and teaching skills.

EXAMPLE OF AN E-LEARNING TEAM

Let's look at at an example of the team required for a couple of projects. First we'll look at the roster of talent required for a large, complex effort. Then we'll see how to trim those requirements to fit the needs of a smaller, simpler project.

Team for a Large, Complex E-Learning Project

Table 10-1 lists the team members needed for a large, complex e-learning project. This project might involve creating an extensive course or even a series of related courses. It would incorporate a variety of media, rich interactivity, extensive tracking, and live Webcast lectures and other presentations.

Downsizing to Fit the Needs of a Simpler Project

Your project may not need all the skills listed in table 10-1. In fact, not all the people listed there need be in one organization, and it is possible that the same required skills can be provided by different combinations of team members. If your project is only moderately complex, you can whittle down the roster considerably. Let's suppose you are creating a course of moderate length, say a few hours. Your course will have a facilitator who communicates with learners through email and a discussion forum. Because not all learners have high-speed network connections, you choose to limit your use of rich media.

Start at the top. Can you find an instructional designer with enough business experience to serve as project leader and lead designer? And, can this person handle all design tasks, eliminating the need for subordinate module designers? Perhaps you can find a candidate for lead designer with enough technical skills to handle course integration. Consolidating these leadership roles saves money and reduces meetings, memos, and other "administrivia."

Because your use of media is constrained by bandwidth, you may be able to have a single person create the necessary graphics and other media. Look for

Table 10-1. Who's on the e-learning team?

Team Member		Role and Responsibilities
Managing the Project	**Project Leader**	• Negotiates overall project goals with upper management and customers • Sets the specific business and learning objectives for the project • Divides the project into specific jobs and tasks, schedules and budgets them, and tracks their completion • Recruits and hires team members
Designing the Course	**Lead Designer**	• Selects and articulates instructional strategies and tactics to accomplish the learning objectives • Researches the needs and preferences of targeted learners • Works with technical specialists to select appropriate technology • Specifies a strategy for creating reusable components and enunciates a rapid development methodology • Specifies layouts, color schemes, typography, and other important aspects of the user-interface and incorporates these choices into templates
	Module Designers	• Design lessons and other course modules • Negotiate objectives with the lead designer • Specify the submodules or combinations of presentation, practice, and feedback necessary to accomplish the objectives
	Subject Matter Experts	• Identify critical concepts and metrics of success • Contribute raw material • Answer questions of designers

continued on page 106

Table 10-1. Who's on the e-learning team? (continued)

Team Member	Role and Responsibilities
Course Integrator	• Uses software tools selected for the project to assemble components into a whole • Creates the menus, map, and other parts of the course framework into which the various lessons, topics, and other modules are assembled • Tests the assembled components to ensure they work as planned
Writers	• Write all original text for display or voice narration • Edit materials contributed by others • Ensure that all verbal material is tuned for its purpose and medium
Graphics Specialists	• Draw original artwork • Ensure that graphics work effectively on the screen and download quickly
Multimedia Developers	• Produce the required animation clips, voice narration sequences, background music, video clips, and other advanced media • Ensure that these components play smoothly and download efficiently
HTML/ XML Coders	• Write required HTML templates, style sheets, XML document type definitions • Fine-tune material created by authoring tools • Create templates and other components for use in authoring tools
Programmers	• Write browser scripts in JavaScript or VBScript • Develop Java applets, ActiveX controls, and like components • Write server programs to process learner's inputs and generate custom pages

Building Content

Category	Role	Responsibilities
Providing the Technical Infrastructure	**Network/Server Administrators**	• Provide the network connections for inside-the-company learners • Set up and maintain the server to host e-learning
	Server/Database Programmers	• Write Active Server pages, Java Server pages, and other server components to interact with learners, track data, access databases, and interface with other corporate systems
	Technical Support Specialists	• Help learners set up their computers for e-learning, connect to the network, install software, and overcome technical problems
Conducting E-learning	**Administrator (Curriculum)**	• Announces courses • Registers learners, collects fees, and answers registration questions • Maintains enrollment records
	Course Facilitator	• Helps learners complete the course • Answers subject matter questions from learners • Moderates online discussions and chat sessions • Motivates discouraged learners
	Online Instructor	• Prepares and presents material in live, online sessions • Operates conferencing tools to stage live, interactive presentations • Answers questions and discusses subject matter with learners

a graphic artist with some multimedia-authoring experience or a multimedia-author with good visual-design skills.

Your next opportunity to consolidate roles is in the technical area. If you keep your design simple, you may not need a lot of hand-coded HTML or custom programming. What you do need can be provided by a single technical specialist, who can assist the lead designer with course integration. Network, server, and technical support may be provided by your IT department or outsourced (see chapter 11).

Because your course does not use live presentations, you do not need an instructor. And, because facilitation is done through email and discussion forums, one facilitator may be able to assist many more students than an instructor could teach. By enabling students to self-register and by automating many of the administrative functions, you may be able to get by with a part-time administrator.

Throughout this example you can see three tactics for fitting the staffing requirements to the scope of your project:

- Simplify your course design to reduce the requirement for technical and media specialists.
- Consolidate job functions by finding multitalented individuals who can fill two or three roles.
- Outsource, first within your own company (the IT department, for example), and then to other companies (see chapter 11).

YOUR TURN

E-learning requires a wide range of skills, knowledge, talent, and viewpoints. The success of your e-learning project depends on assembling the right team. Who will make up your team? Using worksheet 10-1, make a list of the ideal team members for a project you are planning. For each of the functions required for your project, specify the job title and ideal person for the job. Do not be afraid to assign the same job title and person to multiple functions or to assign multiple people to a single complex function.

Worksheet 10-1. Selecting the right people for your e-learning team.

Managing the Project			
Responsibility	Required for Your Project? (✔)	Requirements	Ideal Person for the Job
Business Management			
Project Management			

Designing the Course			
Responsibility	Required for Your Project? (✔)	Requirements	Ideal Person for the Job
Overall Design Integration			
Instructional Design			
Software Architecture			
User-Interface Design			
Subject Matter Expertise			
Knowledge of Buyers of Training			
Knowledge of Learners			

Building Content			
Responsibility	Required for Your Project? (✔)	Requirements	Ideal Person for the Job
Course Integration			
Writing			
Graphics			
Multimedia Development			
HTML and XML Coding			
Browser Scripting			
Server Scripting			
Content Scripting			

Providing the Technical Infrastructure			
Responsibility	Required for Your Project? (✔)	Requirements	Ideal Person for the Job
Network Engineering and Administration			
Server Administration			
Database Connectivity			
Technical Support			

Conducting E-Learning			
Responsibility	Required for Your Project? (✔)	Requirements	Ideal Person for the Job
Curriculum Administration			
Facilitation			
Live Instruction			

11

Where Can You Find Help?

If moving to e-learning seems overwhelming, remember that no one person, one department, or even one company has to do all the work. Get someone else to do the parts of the work that do not take full advantage of your capabilities and resources. Hire, buy, lease, contract, and borrow the advice, labor, skills, tools, technologies, and services you need. This chapter will point out resources that can assist you. (You may also want to consult chapter 14, which provides additional resources for answering your questions and learning more about e-learning.)

How Much Do You Want to Do Yourself?

To make the best use of your skills and talents, you must decide what your organization's goal is for e-learning. Is your goal to deliver training, to develop original training, or to assist others in these tasks? Are you most concerned with means or ends? Where along the spectrum in figure 11-1 do you and your organization want to be?

If your focus is primarily on ends, you may want to subcontract out as much of the work as possible and focus, not on technology, but on delivering training. To reside at the left end of the spectrum, you must be good at evaluating the people and organizations you will rely on to do the work for you. Organizations on the other end of the scale focus on means. They develop tools for others to use. This end is steeped in technology and requires high technical skills to evaluate and implement technologies. Lying in between is a range of options. Options to the left require less work on your part and less technical knowledge, but offer less control over the precise form of the resulting training products.

Figure 11-1. Where is your organization on the spectrum of e-learning?

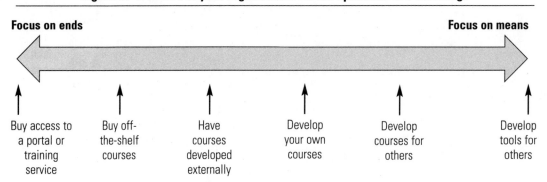

Focus on ends					Focus on means
Buy access to a portal or training service	Buy off-the-shelf courses	Have courses developed externally	Develop your own courses	Develop courses for others	Develop tools for others

WHO CAN HELP?

Once you have decided where to focus your efforts, you can go looking for help. Many people and organizations are willing to offer help—usually for a price. Who are these helpful folks and what can they offer? Keep in mind that many companies may offer both products and services. If you like a product but lack resources to use it yourself, ask if its vendor or someone else offers complementary services.

Information Technology Department

Most large organizations include an IT department to manage their computer and network resources. If your organization has an IT department, involve it in your e-learning effort.

Why involve IT? Although you may not need the assistance of the IT staff, you do not want their opposition. Even if you outsource e-learning, the e-learning content must flow through corporate networks and must pass through corporate firewalls. At least get the IT department's endorsement of your plan.

Besides, the IT department has plenty to offer you. The IT department knows what technologies are in place and what standards and procedures exist for acquiring new technology. In some organizations, the IT department may actually run and control such resources. The IT department can help you select the technologies you need. People in the IT department can provide advice and standards to help you select

- workstations and servers
- operating systems
- server software
- development tools
- programming languages

■ browsers
■ plug-ins.

They can help review products, assessing their reliability, interoperability, and coding quality. Expertise in information technology can prove invaluable in dealing with external suppliers, especially when negotiating licensing agreements.

The IT staff can help you extend available tools. They can suggest system integrators, consultants, and others who can help with your projects. They may be able to do some custom programming or script writing.

As we have said, e-learning can be a complex software development effort. The IT department has experience implementing complex enterprise-level systems mixing multiple hardware and software components. They also may possess expertise in linking your e-learning system to HR, enterprise resource planning, and knowledge management systems that are in place or under way.

The IT department can be a powerful political ally in selling e-learning to the organization and its management. The IT staff offers credibility with executives on matters involving the use of IT to improve productivity. And, they are potentially enthusiastic supporters of e-learning. Some of the most successful deployments of e-learning have been to teach IT skills to IT staff. So, how do you work with the IT department? Check out these suggestions:

■ Involve the IT department early. Find out what services they offer and what they consider their responsibilities.
■ Draft a complete, detailed set of functional requirements, specifying what you need to accomplish, but not exactly which technologies to use.
■ Work actively with IT to identify the best technologies to meet your functional requirements. You may not be a technical expert, but you may know more about e-learning software than the IT department does initially.
■ Learn of any corporate standards that may constrain your choice of approach or rule out specific products. Make sure, for instance, that firewalls will not screen out any media you are planning to use.
■ Work with the IT department to decide who will be responsible for which tasks and technologies. For example, who will manage and maintain the server hosting the training?

Be understanding if the IT staff seem skeptical at first. They may not view e-learning as a valid use of corporate IT resources. The IT department may fear that they will be saddled with problems caused by your use of tools and technologies not tested on the corporate network. Your efforts could clog their networks, overload their servers, and reduce the reliability of critical enterprise systems for which they are responsible. In particular, the bandwidth required for e-learning might swamp an already strapped intranet.

System Integrators

Although individual hardware and software components are easy enough to operate, getting all the components required for a complete project can require a vast range of technical skills—needed only at the beginning of the project. That's where a system integrator comes in.

The system integrator combines the pieces and gets them working together on your organization's network. System integrators are best for big projects and the big-name firms may be best qualified for very large projects. Examples of some big name system integrators providing learning solutions include Arthur Andersen (www.aavln.com), IBM (www.ibm.com), and EDS (www.eds.com). Before contacting a system integrator, decide how much or how little of their services you need. Also, specify the results that you want to achieve. Talk to some of their customers who have requested solutions similar to your own. For the system integrators you consider, ask yourself:

- How well do they listen?
- Will they develop a solution customized for your organization or just reuse one from a previous project?
- Can they work with your IT department or technical staff?

Borrow From Other Departments

Do not overlook the talent and skills available in other parts of your larger organization. If you do not need a person full-time, perhaps you can borrow him or her from a sister department. Accomplished writers, editors, and visual artists may hide out in corporate communications and marketing departments. Advertising may have a bevy of animators, voice narrators, and video producers. Accounting may be willing to help you count your beans and manage your spreadsheet. Classroom instructors in your own department may be willing to put in some overtime in exchange for developing marketable e-learning skills. Before you hire from the outside, borrow from down the hall.

Consultants

The term consultant has a broad range of meanings. In this context, consultants are people who give advice, suggest alternatives, test prototypes, and research special issues for you. Consultants provide independent, knowledgeable advice and design services. They can help you answer design and technical questions and perform a reality check on your plans and expectations.

First, identify the expertise you need, then find a consultant in that specialty. Start by asking a colleague for a recommendation. You can also search the Web for "consultant e-learning" or equivalent terms. Many professional organizations maintain directories of consultants.

When considering consultants, ask yourself these questions:

- Is the consultant truly independent, or is he or she financially linked to particular tool suppliers, systems integrators, or other service providers?
- Does the consultant have a balance of professional credentials and practical experience?
- Can the consultant supply samples of his or her work?

■ Is the consultant a good listener?

■ Does the consultant really understand your goals and concerns?

Realize that many consultants work under nondisclosure agreements, making it hard to check references. Instead, check for publications and presentations they have made.

Make sure you understand the consultant's rate structure up front and negotiate a contract that makes effective use of his or her efforts. (Warning: The author of this book is a consultant. You may want to consider that fact as you read this section.)

Course Development Firms

Course development firms create e-learning to your specifications, freeing you from the task of hiring and supervising a multidisciplinary team. To find course developers, search the Web for "WBT, e-learning, course developer" or equivalent terms. When picking a course developer, ask yourself these questions:

■ Does the course developer have instructional design expertise?

■ Can the developer use the media you specify and deliver in the file formats you require, or is the developer limited to a specific authoring tool?

■ How much experience does the developer have with e-learning?

■ Can the developer work within your constraints of bandwidth, budget, and schedule?

Course developers need clear instructions and specifications on what to create. Fill in any details you believe should not be left to the judgment of the course developer. Be prepared to provide the developer with as much course material as possible in electronic format, including illustrations, logos, audio and video recordings, and so forth.

Multimedia Developers

Multimedia developers create specific content modules, such as illustrations, animation sequences, sound effects, musical backgrounds, and video clips. They may also provide interactive multimedia components and some custom scripting services. Multimedia developers can provide esoteric technical skills needed on a short-term basis or just for a particular project. To find multimedia developers, search the Web for "multimedia developer" or equivalent terms.

Pick developers with the specialized expertise you need—a particular tool, file format, or medium. When considering multimedia developers, ask questions like these:

■ Can they match the desired tone or style, or do they have their own distinctive style?

■ Can they work within your constraints of bandwidth, budget, and schedule?

■ Do they balance creativity, technical skill, and dependability?

Develop a detailed specification for each content module the developer is to create. Be specific about limitations of dimensions, file size, colors, and file formats. Provide samples of other content with which the module is to be consistent.

Application Service Providers

Application service providers (ASPs) offer Web-hosting as well as the services of consultants, systems integrators, course developers, and multimedia producers.

> ## Contract for Specific Media Skills
>
> If you sporadically need a specific media skill, such as copyediting, technical writing, voice narration, illustration, or animation, consider hiring an independent contractor. To find some, search the Web for the name of the skill you want combined with the words "freelance" or "independent contractor" or combinations of these terms.

The term *application service provider* generally refers to a Website from which you subscribe to and run application programs. They let customers rent rather than own infrastructure and content. You should note, however, that the terms ASP and portal are so new and used so loosely that it is often hard to tell them apart. Also, many companies combine the characteristics of both. For the sake of this book, the main distinction is that the portal offers courses of its choosing, and an ASP offers services of your choosing. In contrast to portals, ASPs offer more services, customize offerings more extensively, and let their customers participate in development.

In the training arena, the term ASP has a somewhat broader meaning covering a wider range of services including hosting, course management, collaboration services, and content development tools. In fact, ASPs that specialize in learning services and content sometimes call themselves learning services providers.

To find examples of ASPs specializing in e-learning, search the Web for "application service provider" and "training." Some examples of e-learning ASPs include DigitalThink (www.digitalthink.com), GeoLearning (www .geolearning.com), MindLever.com, and SocratEase (www.eutectics.com).

Why use an ASP? They provide a simpler approach than owning and operating tools yourself. By using an ASP, you have less software to buy, load, and upgrade. They require less of an up-front financial commitment and less technical expertise. You can buy just as much service as you need.

Services offered by ASPs include hosting of e-learning developed or purchased by your organization; specialized learning facilities such as virtual meeting rooms, chat sessions, and discussion forums; experts to help develop or purchase courses; tools for authoring courses; and technical and administrative support. Some can even set up a private learning portal just for your organization.

Usually ASPs work best for small organizations that cannot immediately afford the costs and time to develop and deploy their own learning infrastructure, but who do need control over course content, either by developing or purchasing courses.

When evaluating ASPs, try out their services to determine the reliability of their servers, staff responsiveness, ease of use of their products, and the quality of their services. Also check their references. Talk to long-term and recent customers. For the ASPs under consideration, ask these questions:

- Do they provide all the services you need?
- Do you pay for only the services you use?
- Do their services restrict course design?
- How much can they maintain the corporate look of your courses?
- How reliable are their services in terms of uptime?
- How long have they been in business?
- Who are their major customers?

If all you need is someone to host the e-learning you develop, you probably do not need a full-blown ASP. Consider instead using a Web-hosting service. To find a Web-hosting service search the Web for "Web-hosting service," "network service provider," and "Internet service provider."

Training Portals

A training portal is a Website offering access to training courses. Some experts restrict the term *portal* to sites that merely help learners find training available on other sites. Other experts use the term for sites that provide training content right on the same site.

In any case, portals make training services available through a single Website. Some portals offer a wide variety of general courses, and others focus on the needs of a particular industry. Most do so by aggregating content from separate developers or suppliers. Some may provide additional services, such as learning management systems, discussion and chat services, tech support, and coaching for subject areas.

Behind some portals, the courses all look and behave the same. Behind others, each course is unique. This is because some portals develop their own courses or at least have required templates and standards developers must follow. Others just collect courses developed separately by independent suppliers.

One advantage of training portals is that they provide immediate access to courses without any development costs on your part. Portals also take care of maintenance and updating of courses. They also provide privacy for employees who do not want their learning activities tracked internally.

Portals work best for organizations that lack the resources to develop their own courses and training infrastructure but whose training needs can be satisfied by existing e-learning courses. The primary advantage to portals may be the price of learning. The prices for learning portals can range from $10 to $1,000 per learner per course. Keep in mind that even prices at the upper end of this scale may be less than the cost of custom development on your part.

Examples of training portals can be found by searching the Web for that term. Some better known training portals include VerticalNet (www.vertical net.com), Learn2.com (www.learn2.com), Headlight.com, Thinq (learning .thinq.com), DDI (www.ddi-usa.com), Vital Learning (www.vitallearning.com), and NETg (www.netg.com).

When considering a portal, ask to see a wide sample of the courses you are considering. If possible, test the effectiveness of these courses with sample learners. As you consider each candidate, ask:

- Will their courses meet your objectives?
- Are their courses of consistently high quality?
- Do their billing terms fit your situation? That is, do they bill by the course, by student, or by subscription to a range of courses?
- Do they develop their own courses or buy from others?
- What record keeping and tracking services do they offer?
- Can you customize the appearance of their courses to fit your corporate identity?

E-Learners

One of the best and most often overlooked sources of help is the people being trained. Learners can provide valuable assistance as you develop and deploy e-learning. Involving learners emphasizes that they are partners in the learning process. What are some of the ways learners can help producers of e-learning? Here are a few suggestions:

- Set up a support discussion group where learners can help one another. Give extra credit for such efforts.
- Use student projects as examples, optional readings, or baseline content in the next version of the course.
- Assign learners responsibility for moderating discussion forums.
- Have learners develop presentations or complete lessons on various aspects of the subject.
- Encourage learners to submit corrections to any errors they spot in the course.

How Do You Screen Suppliers?

To put together an effective solution, you will have to talk to suppliers of products, services, and advice. How can you make sure they listen to you and speak your language?

First make sure you are talking to someone knowledgeable. Ask how long the sales representative has been with the company and what e-learning experience he or she has. Has the representative actually used the product or service? To escape canned sales pitches and focus the discussion on your needs, continually ask, "So what?" Insist that suppliers translate the features of their products into benefits that apply to your project. To that end, prepare a concise statement of your goals. Ask how the suppliers can help you meet these goals.

Your Turn

Spend a few minutes deciding what tasks you and your organization can delegate or subcontract. Then, using worksheet 11-1, write a statement of goals, spelling out exactly what you want to accomplish in your e-learning effort. Do not be too specific about how you want to accomplish this goal. Have suppliers specify how they can help you accomplish this goal.

Worksheet 11-1. How can suppliers help meet your organizational goals?
Our goal is to . . .
How can this supplier help you accomplish this goal?

How much do you want to do yourself? List in worksheet 11-2 the major tasks necessary to create and deploy e-learning in your organization. Now check off the ones you or your organization can handle. For each unchecked task, decide where you will find help.

Worksheet 11-2. Determining which tasks can be done internally and which can be done by others.

Major Task	Performed Internally? (Yes/No)	Others Who Can Perform This Task

12

How Do You Launch Your Effort?

Now it is time to put the pieces together and get your organization moving toward e-learning. Such a grand endeavor requires a plan. Although this chapter points out the main steps to include in your plan, it is deliberately incomplete. It is an outline for you to fill in as you create your strategic plan for e-learning. If you did the action items at the end of each chapter, you have already done much of the work necessary to assemble your plan.

OVERVIEW OF A PLAN

Figure 12-1 shows the structure of a plan for moving to e-learning. This structure is explained throughout the rest of this chapter.

Figure 12-1. A plan for moving to e-learning.

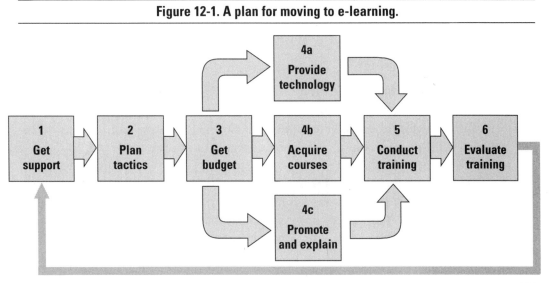

Although this structure may not apply exactly to your situation, you can use it as a model as you draft your own plan. Remember to specify who will perform each task and when.

Step 1: Get Broad, High-Level Support

With both executive and grassroots support, your e-learning effort will proceed more smoothly and rapidly than if it is perceived as a renegade effort by techno-fanatics. The first step, then, is to communicate the advantages of e-learning to all those who will be affected by the move to e-learning.

One approach to garner needed support is to call a meeting of the primary stakeholders. Set the goal as one of establishing a common vision for e-learning in the organization. The agenda for the meeting should call for the participants to

■ agree on the need for e-learning
■ set strategic e-learning goals in terms of what percentage of training will be e-learning five years from now
■ select initial projects for the next couple of years
■ elect an e-learning leader and implementation team for these projects.

For this meeting, invite heads of the major training organizations within the organization. Do not forget to include representatives of field and foreign offices involved in training. Also, secure participation by high-level executives from the HR and IT departments. If participants are not knowledgeable about e-learning, provide them with reading materials and access to sample courses before the meeting.

Step 2: Plan Tactics for Introducing E-Learning

Once you have an empowered team in place, you can begin translating lofty ambitions into pragmatic action. The next step is to develop a detailed plan for your first e-learning projects. The following section spells out the steps for creating your detailed plan.

Spell Out Immediate Goals. Agree on and clearly state your initial business and learning goals. Over the next year or two, what groups of people will you train? What knowledge, skills, or attitudes will they gain from your e-learning? And what will be the business and financial results of the training?

Analyze Your Target Consumers. Consumers of training include both those who buy training and those who take training. Sometimes they are the same but not always. The buyers are typically the managers of groups to be trained. Try to identify the people who actually make purchasing or enrollment decisions. Learners are those who will take e-learning. Keep in mind that these may not be the same people who are taking classroom training now. Use focus groups, survey questionnaires, telephone interviews, and other techniques to cover a range of critical demographic characteristics (such as age, gender, language skills, and degree of motivation) at least as broad as those of your target learners.

Agree on Tactics. Once everyone agrees on the goals, you can begin developing a detailed tactical plan. Here is a checklist of the decisions you should make before proceeding:

- What are your financial goals—to make money, break even, or offer e-learning at a loss?
- Will you charge participating departments? Will you charge per learner, per amount accessed, per learner–per course, or some other unit? Or will you offer a library-card or open-enrollment plan?
- How will you acquire courses? Who will design the courses? Who will build them? Or, will you contract with a portal for access to their courses?
- How will courses be evaluated and updated?
- How will you track learner performance? What measures of performance will you record? Who will have access to these data?
- Who will provide technical support for learners?
- What form of e-learning will you use? Will learners interact with just the computer? With each other? With a facilitator?
- What skills and knowledge will learners need to take e-learning?
- What team members will you need?

Specify Courses. Before you can estimate development costs or search for potential courses, you need a detailed specification of the courses you plan to offer. This will require expanding the statement of learning goals to make clear the required scope, instructional methods, and other required characteristics of the e-learning.

Deal With Potential Problems. Identify potential roadblocks, such as legal, privacy, and security concerns, and get someone working on them. Brainstorm to list all the things that could go wrong. Find solutions or workarounds for any problems that could cause your project to fail.

Step 3: Get a Budget

Deploying e-learning can be expensive, especially your first few projects. Before undertaking expensive development efforts or signing long-term licensing agreements, estimate the total costs and get funding. Where can you find the required funding?

Enroll internal investors. Ask other departments to share the costs of deploying e-learning. Will internal departments underwrite the costs of training that they need? Will the IT department bear the costs of providing necessary technical infrastructure?

Try borrowing from existing programs. If e-learning will reduce the costs of conventional classroom training, you may be able to use some of the anticipated savings to pay for initial development of e-learning. Another possibility is to borrow against future earnings. If your e-learning courses will generate revenue, you may be able to borrow against these future revenues.

Step 4a: Provide Needed Technology

As pointed out in chapter 9, e-learning requires extensive technology to author, to host, and to access. You must ensure that all participants in e-learning have the hardware, software, and network connections required by their roles. Don't forget that you must ensure that participants have access to technical support to answer questions and resolve problems that might occur.

If you are developing your own courses, you must ensure that developers have the workstations and other tools to author courses. Likewise, if you are hosting courses internally, you must set up the necessary servers. And, if you are offering courses to internal staff, you must ensure that they have the computers and workstations necessary to take the courses.

Step 4b: Acquire Courses

You must translate your specifications for courses into real courses ready for learners to take. You have three main choices:

- You can design and build the courses yourself.
- You can design the courses and have someone else build them.
- You can buy, license, or subscribe to courses developed by others.

Regardless of how you acquire the courses, remember to test them to ensure that they accomplish your learning objectives.

Step 4c: Explain and Promote

Even potentially effective e-learning can fail if unenthusiastic producers force it upon unprepared learners. As you prepare to offer e-learning, take steps to ensure a receptive welcome.

■ Identify early targets for e-learning.

■ Go public with your plans. Announce your e-learning strategy.

■ Dispel rumors and myths about e-learning. Reassure everyone that classroom training will not vanish until e-learning has proven itself.

■ Point out the advantages of e-learning to all. Share testimonials from e-learners and letters of support from high executives.

■ Convince important decision makers, especially the managers of potential trainees.

Step 5: Conduct Training

Your first attempts at offering e-learning are your riskiest. Take extra steps to get learners started right and to keep them motivated and productive. Some steps you can take to ensure that your first class is successful include these:

■ *Train the roll-out team.* Make sure that all involved in the first offering have the knowledge, skills, and attitudes to carry out their roles. Meet frequently with facilitators, support technicians, moderators, and administrators to ensure that they are ready.

■ *Schedule getting-started briefings for learners.* Even though your courses may be self-directed, schedule a face-to-face meeting with initial learners to welcome them and overcome any concerns they may have.

■ *Publish instructions for getting started.* Make sure that learners know how to take e-learning. Do not expect them to remember everything. Publish a complete guide. Give it to learners on paper and make updates available from your Website.

■ *Provide telephone support.* Let learners know that help is available. Do not let them fail.

Step 6: Evaluate Training

Learn from your efforts. Evaluate the effectiveness of your e-learning offerings. Did learners complete the courses? Would they recommend them to co-workers? Did they actually learn what you intended? Did they learn what they intended? Are they applying what they learned to their jobs and to their lives? Did the courses accomplish their business objectives as well as their learning objectives?

Do not lose momentum. Build on your success and on lessons learned. Plow back what you learned from your first efforts into revisions of these offerings and into future offerings. With each e-learning effort, improve your design, techniques, and technology.

YOUR TURN

Using this chapter as a model, outline your own plan in worksheet 12-1. Have knowledgeable associates critique the plan. When you are satisfied, start acting on the plan.

In drafting your own plan, feel free to cross out items, add items, or redraw the plan entirely. As each item is completed, check it off.

Worksheet 12-1. Develop your own plan for launching an e-learning effort.

Step 1: Get Support			
Task	**Person Responsible**	**Due Date**	**Done? (✔)**
Get high-level and grassroots support for your project			
Other:			
Other:			

Step 2: Plan Tactics for Introducing E-Learning			
Task	**Person Responsible**	**Due Date**	**Done? (✔)**
Spell out immediate goals			
Agree on tactics			
Specify courses			
Deal with potential problems			
Other:			
Other:			

Step 3: Get a Budget			
Task	**Person Responsible**	**Due Date**	**Done? (✔)**
Estimate the total costs			
Obtain funding			
Other:			
Other:			

Step 4a: Provide Needed Technology			
Task	**Person Responsible**	**Due Date**	**Done? (✔)**
For developers of e-learning			
For hosting e-learning			
For consumers of e-learning			
Other:			
Other:			

Step 4b: Acquire Courses			
Task	**Person Responsible**	**Due Date**	**Done? (✔)**
Design and build your own courses			
Buy, license, or subscribe to courses by others			
Other:			
Other:			

Step 4c: Explain and Promote			
Task	**Person Responsible**	**Due Date**	**Done? (✔)**
Announce your plans			
Dispel rumors and myths			
Point out advantages of e-learning			
Convince decision makers			
Other:			
Other:			
Step 5: Conduct Training			
Task	**Person Responsible**	**Due Date**	**Done? (✔)**
Train the roll-out team			
Brief initial e-learners			
Publish getting-started instructions			
Provide telephone support			
Other:			
Other:			
Step 6: Evaluate Training			
Task	**Person Responsible**	**Due Date**	**Done? (✔)**
Objectively evaluate the course			
Apply what your evaluation tells you to redesigning the course			

13

How Do You Deploy E-Learning Strategically?

E-learning is a momentous change. Nevertheless, e-learning should be an end in itself, as learning is just part of larger changes sweeping business and society. Now you can step back and see how e-learning fits into this bigger picture.

HOW DOES E-LEARNING PROMOTE A NEW MODEL FOR TRAINING?

Over the past 20 years or so, a new way of thinking about training has emerged. Training is no longer seen as a form of publishing; it is now considered an organizational catalyst.

The Publishing Model

The publishing model—or broadcast model as it is sometimes known—underlies the operations of most training and publishing organizations worldwide. At the center of the publishing model is the producer. The producer may be a developer of training, a teacher in the classroom, or an author of books and manuals. The producer works by consulting the enlightened few (figure 13-1). These are the experts who have the knowledge needed by others. The producer gathers this knowledge, organizes it, and expresses it. The producer then distributes or publishes the information to the ignorant masses.

The publishing model is orderly, efficient, and ubiquitous. It works superbly for teaching fixed or slowly evolving knowledge to large groups of people.

The Catalyst Model

The catalyst model is more sophisticated—and considerably messier. This model still involves a knowledge producer, and it still involves those who need

Figure 13-1. The "publishing" model of training.

The enlightened few
The ignorant masses

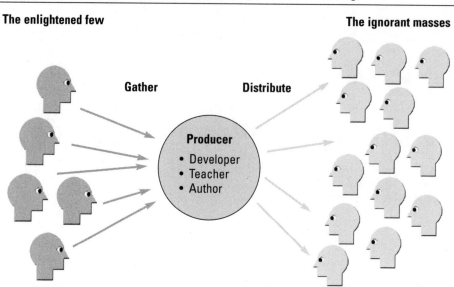

the knowledge. But now, the exchange with knowledge consumers is a two-way exchange. Consumers can ask questions and may even contribute ideas themselves. Every student is a teacher and every teacher, a student.

Some knowledge consumers also become knowledge producers themselves. These local-area experts exchange information with a subcommunity of the knowledge consumers, such as those interested in an esoteric issue of the overall subject or those concerned with how one particular department applies the knowledge (figure 13-2). In the catalyst model, knowledge consumers are no longer isolated. They discuss, they chat, and they exchange email furiously. These circumferential exchanges complement the radial exchanges that center on the producer.

What does this new model imply for the producers? They must conduct dialogs with their consumers and not merely broadcast information. They must develop materials to foster and support local-area experts. They must put in place communications mechanisms that allow consumers to communicate with one another, with local-area experts, and with them.

HOW DOES E-LEARNING SUPPORT KNOWLEDGE MANAGEMENT?

Knowledge management can be defined simply as the ways a group of people makes itself smarter. The relationship with training is clear. Training educates individuals; knowledge management educates entire organizations and populations. The group of people educated may be the employees of Royal Widgit

Figure 13-2. The "catalyst" model of training.

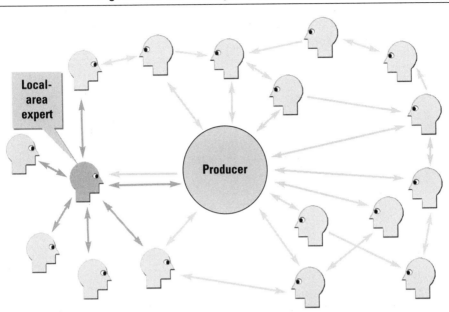

Limited, or it may be the students of Lightspeed University, or it may be the customers and potential customers of BlottoBlaster Software.

Knowledge management has many parts, including activities such as publications management, information repositories, data mining, collaboration systems, process reengineering, best practices, competency measurement, resource catalogs, and, indisputably, training. Training is legitimately an essential part of any knowledge management effort (figure 13-3). But training does not cover the whole of knowledge management.

E-learning provides a logical starting point for future development of more comprehensive knowledge management programs. Because it is electronic and network-based, it can use the same infrastructure and communication mechanisms as other parts of knowledge management, making connecting them much easier. How do organizations manage knowledge, and how can e-learning contribute to these processes? Consider some of the ways e-learning can help groups of people become collectively and individually smarter (table 13-1).

HOW DOES E-LEARNING CONTRIBUTE TO THE KNOWLEDGE ECONOMY?

The world is transforming itself into a global knowledge economy where success depends more on knowledge than on labor and capital. All products and services today have a knowledge component. The size of this component is growing and may soon dominate in even the most traditional products and services.

Figure 13-3. Role of training in knowledge management.

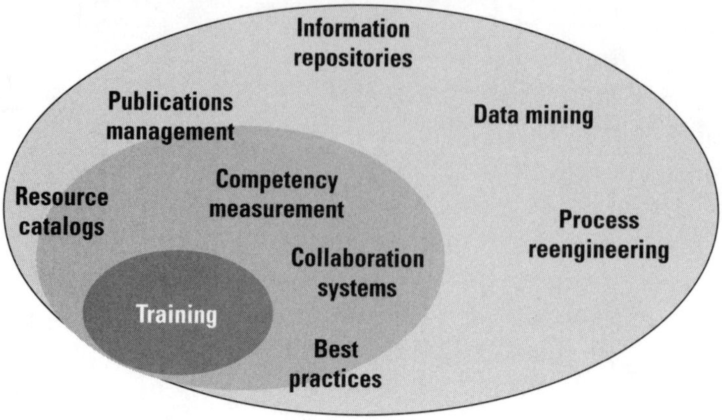

Among developed countries, more than half the gross domestic product comes from production and distribution of knowledge by workers paid more for using their brains than their muscles. This does not imply that labor and capital are not important in a knowledge economy, only that they are not the most critical factors. Many workers still tote and lift, but more are paid to think, plan, design, and communicate.

Table 13-1. How e-learning supports knowledge management.

Knowledge Management Process	How E-Learning Can Contribute
Increasing the knowledge of individuals	Allows anybody in the organization to learn whatever they need anywhere, anytime
Capturing knowledge in a reusable form	Captures knowledge for easy distribution and use
Refining knowledge	Teaches advanced subjects to promote more sophisticated thinking about those subjects
	Can be used to teach how to analyze, edit, and sharpen knowledge
Sharing knowledge	Demonstrates and teaches how to share knowledge and skills by incorporating collaboration mechanisms
	Stresses job-related skills
Applying knowledge to solve problems	Can use simulations to prepare learners to apply concepts learned in training
	Can monitor posttraining application of knowledge via collaborative mechanisms

Increasingly, it is the unique knowledge of the organization that is most important in determining its success. Without good ideas there would be no company to attract venture capital or to hire janitors. Companies with better knowledge about their customers, their business, and their employees stay ahead of their competition.

Knowledge economies produce knowledge products and services. Commonly cited examples include high-technology products such as computer hardware, computer software, mobile phones, and other telecommunications products. But, traditional industrial products, such as automobiles and airplanes, are fast transforming themselves into knowledge products, too. Today, the most powerful computer system owned by most families is the one parked in their driveway or garage. Even mid-priced automobiles include complex networks of computers controlling the low-emissions engine, the antilock brakes, the automatic transmission, and even the heater. Upscale models include satellite navigation displays and built-in wireless communications systems.

At the core of the knowledge economy are knowledge workers. What do these knowledge workers require and what should employers require of them? Perhaps the best answer comes from management guru Peter Drucker (1994): "They [knowledge workers] require a great deal of formal education and the ability to acquire and to apply theoretical and analytical knowledge. They require a different approach to work and a different mind-set. Above all, they require a habit of continuous learning."

How are these things to be provided? E-learning would be the logical choice to deliver such continuous learning.

WHAT IS THE FUTURE OF E-LEARNING?

E-learning today is crude, clumsy, and inefficient—much like classroom learning was back in the days when it consisted of sitting on wooden benches for hours listening to someone read from the school's only copy of a book. E-learning is evolving into forms that little resemble its crude beginnings. Here are a few fearless predictions of what e-learning may offer:

- *Technology will become more powerful yet less visible.* Computers and communication technologies will continue to grow faster, more powerful, and cheaper. Software will become simpler. In 1995, creating a Webpage required learning HTML. Today dozens of Webpage-editing programs write the code for you. Technology will become less and less of a constraint to designers of training as they focus their efforts on innovation and quality.
- *The classroom and books will be reborn.* E-learning will not replace classroom training or paper books. To the contrary, by relieving them of tasks

they do not do well, e-learning could spark a burst of innovation in these venerable forms.

■ *An educational free market will emerge.* As e-learning and e-commerce get together, a global free market of training will develop. Suppliers with highly effective courses and other knowledge products will thrive. Competition will keep prices in line and quality high.

■ *Learning will be omnipresent.* The optical fiber networks, communication satellites, and wireless devices mean that soon learning opportunities will be everywhere. The notion of having to go to a specific place to learn something will seem quaint to our grandchildren and bizarre to their grandchildren.

■ *Learning will be continual throughout life.* Today, continual learning means popping back to the university to take the odd course every year or so. In the future learning will be almost continuous. Although long, formal classes will still exist, much learning will occur during spare moments in five-minute bites.

■ *Training on all subjects will be universally accessible.* As e-learning technologies are simplified, more and more individuals and organizations will find ways to share their unique expertise. Everyone will become both student and teacher, and learning will be as natural a part of life as eating and breathing.

Your Turn

Take a few moments to peer beyond the immediate goals of e-learning to identify larger benefits that your e-learning can foster and inspire.

The catalyst model of learning differs from the publishing model in some important characteristics. How can you effect these differences to move your training from a publishing model to catalyst model? Try worksheet 13-1.

Worksheet 13-1. Moving toward a catalyst model.	
Difference Between the Catalyst Model and the Publishing Model	**How Can You Move Your Training in This Direction**
Consumers and producers of training communicate frequently and deeply in ways that go beyond simple feedback. Consumers often contribute directly to new e-learning content.	
Consumers of training communicate richly with their peers, many of whom have no direct contact with the producers of training.	
Local-area experts adapt the producer's offerings to the needs of their specific workgroup, team, or industry. Many receive training from such local-area experts rather than from the originator of the e-learning.	

How can your e-learning efforts promote knowledge management in your organization? How would you extend e-learning to provide knowledge management results? Use worksheet 13-2 to record your ideas.

Worksheet 13-2. Knowledge management, anyone?	
Knowledge Management Process	**How Will You Use E-Learning to Contribute to This Process?**
Increasing the knowledge of individuals	
Capturing knowledge in a reusable form	
Refining knowledge	
Sharing knowledge	
Applying knowledge to solve problems	

14

Where Can You Learn More?

If you are ready to start moving your organization into the e-learning age, start now. As you proceed, you may find some of these sources helpful in providing the knowledge and support you need.

WHAT ORGANIZATIONS SHOULD YOU JOIN?

Organizations provide a rich source of expertise, camaraderie, and support. Here are a few organizations active in the movement to e-learning:

ASTD
1640 King Street
Box 1443
Alexandria, Virginia 22313-2043
703.683.8100
http://www.astd.org

International Society for Performance Improvement (ISPI)
1400 Spring Street, Suite 260
Silver Spring, Maryland 20910
301.587.8570
http://www.ispi.org

Society for Applied Learning Technology (SALT)
50 Culpeper Street
Warrenton, Virginia 20186
540.347.0055
http://www.salt.org

WHAT BOOKS SHOULD YOU READ?

You read this book, so perhaps some other books might guide your way. Here are a few that continue the themes started in this one.

The 2000/2001 ASTD Distance Learning Yearbook
K. Mantyla, editor
ASTD, publisher

The ASTD Media Selection Tool for Workplace Learning
R. Marx, author
ASTD, publisher

Designing Web-Based Training
W. Horton, author
John Wiley & Sons, publisher

Distance Learning: A Step-by-Step Guide for Trainers
K. Mantyla, author
ASTD, publisher

Distance Training
D. Schreiber and Z. Berg, editors
Jossey-Bass, publisher

Getting Started with Online Learning
W. Horton, B. Bruce, and C. Fallon, authors
C. Vescia, editor
Macromedia, publisher
Available online at
http://www.macromedia.com/learning/online_learning_guide.pdf

Interactive Distance Learning Exercises That Really Work!
K. Mantyla, author
ASTD, publisher

Managing Web-Based Training.
A. Ellis, E. Wagner, and W. Longmire, authors
ASTD, publisher

A Trainer's Guide to Web-Based Instruction: Getting Started on Intranet- and Internet-Based Training
J. Alden, author
ASTD, publisher

Web-Based Instruction
B.H. Khan, editor
Educational Technology Publications, publisher

Web-Based Training
M. Driscoll, author
Jossey-Bass/Pfeiffer, publisher

WHICH WEBSITES SHOULD YOU VISIT?

Websites dedicated to e-learning can provide examples and detailed information. Here are just a few that focus on the subject of e-learning.

http://www.designingwbt.com
The companion site for the book *Designing Web-Based Training* by W. Horton not only contains most of the examples shown in the book, but also provides design tools such as forms and templates, a sample WBT course, and extensive e-learning reference material.

http://www.influent-rx.com/
The Influent Resource Exchange, sponsored by Influent Technology Group, is a good place to find resources for training, support, and design. Visitors are encouraged to share resources as well.

http://www.masie.com
The Masie Center, an e-learning think tank in Saratoga Springs, New York, has a Website with links to many useful articles and presentations on technology and learning.

http://www.trainingsupersite.com/
The Training Supersite is full of articles, conference lists, and learning links. It is a joint venture of *Training* magazine and Bill Communications.

PERIODICALS, PAPER, AND ONLINE

E-learning has spawned a healthy brood of magazines, ezines, and newsletters. Here are a few that deliver well-researched and current information at reasonable prices:

e-learning magazine
www.elearningmag.com

Learning Circuits, ASTD's online magazine on e-learning
http://www.learningcircuits.com/

Online Learning Magazine
http://www.onlinelearningmag.com/

Training Magazine
http://www.trainingmag.com/

OnLine Learning News
http://www.vnulearning.com/brochure.htm

WHERE CAN YOU ASK QUESTIONS?

One of the best places to find answers to your questions is on the various e-learning discussion groups. As you visit each of these groups, lurk a while to see what kinds of issues are discussed there. Then, join in the conversation and offer your suggestions and opinions to others.

ASTD's virtual community
http://www.astd.org/virtual_community/forums/learning_tech/learning_tech.cgi
ASTD's Web-based virtual community contains discussion threads on the value of e-learning, implementation strategies, tools, suppliers, and a wide range of other related subjects.

Influent Resource Exchange Forum
www.influent-rx.com/
Influent's forums address practical issues in e-learning and other aspects of training and support.

alt.training.technology
news:alt.training.technology
This Internet newsgroup hosts discussions about e-learning technology, announcements of courses and job openings, and academic programs in learning technology.

alt.education.distance
news:alt.education.distance
This Internet newsgroup consists primarily of announcements of university courses and requests for information about such courses. Some e-learning design issues do arise from time to time.

WHAT CONFERENCES SHOULD YOU ATTEND?

Conferences provide great opportunities to meet and speak with the people building e-learning solutions. Many such conventions include workshops, presentations, and product exhibitions. Some of the main annual conferences include these:

ASTD International Conference and Exposition
ASTD, sponsor
http://www.astd.org

Annual Conference on Distance Teaching & Learning
University of Wisconsin-Madison, sponsor
http://www.uwex.edu/disted/conference/

Online Learning Conference and Exposition
Bill Communications and Lakewood Conferences, sponsors
http://www.vnulearning.com

TechKnowledge
ASTD, sponsor
http://www.astd.org

WBT Producer Conference and Expo
Influent Technology Group, sponsor
http://www.influent.com

YOUR TURN

To round out your e-learning knowledge and skills and to keep current, you must identify reliable information sources. Take a few minutes to plan how you will find such sources.

Assemble a personal learning plan. How will you continue to increase your knowledge and skills in e-learning? List in worksheet 14-1 the knowledge and skills you feel you need. Identify sources for learning each. As you acquire each item, enter the date.

Worksheet 14-1. Set up a plan for developing the skills and knowledge you need to implement e-learning.

Skill or Knowledge	Source (organizations, books, conferences, online discussions)	Date Acquired

References

ASK International. (1998). "A New Training Concept, JUST IN TIME." www.ask intl.com/concept.html.

Adams, G.L. (1992, March). "Why Interactive?" *Multimedia & Videodisc Monitor, 10,* 20.

Anonymous. (2000, May). "Does E-Learning Really Work?" *Inside Technology Training,* 14.

ASTD. (2001). *The 2001 ASTD State of the Industry Report.* Alexandria, VA: Author.

Barron, A.E., and C. Rickelman. (1999, May). "Creating an Online Corporate University: Lessons Learned." ASTD's 1999 International Conference & Exposition, Atlanta.

Bradley Associates. (1994). *Multimedia Made Easy: Guide to Developing Interactive Multimedia for Training.* Palo Alto, CA: Author.

Clark, P., and B. Johnson. (1999). "Moving from ILT to E-Learning: A Novell Education Case Study." WBT Producer Conference, San Diego.

Cooper, L. (1999, February). "Anatomy of an Online Course." *T.H.E. Journal, 26.*

Densford, L. (1998, November–December). "Sun Microsystems: Finding New Ways to Put Training in Context." *Corporate University Review, 6.*

Docent. (1999). "Lucent's Wireless University." www.docent.com/solutions/success /lucent.htm.

Drucker, P. (1994, November). "The Age of Social Transformation." *Atlantic Monthly, 274*(5), 53–80. http://www.theatlantic.com/issues/95dec/chilearn /drucker.htm

Fletcher, J.D. (1990). *Effectiveness and Cost of Interactive Videodisc Instruction in Defense Training and Education.* Washington, DC: Institute for Defense Analysis.

Fryer, B. (1998, October). "MCI Goes Live." *Inside Technology Training, 2,* 18–22.

Gillette, B. (1998, October). "Taking Training Online." *Corporate Meetings & Incentives.* www.meetingsnet.com.

Hall, B. (2000a, January–March). "How to Embark on Your E-Learning Adventure." *E-Learning, 1,* 10–16.

Hall, B. (2000b, September). "E-Learning Across the Enterprise." *E-Learning,* 27–34.

IDC. (2000). "Distance Learning in Higher Education: Market Forecast and Analysis, 1999–2004." Framingham, MA: Author. http://www.idc.com:8080/Hardware/press/PR/DMT/DMT121800pr.stm.

Internet Software Consortium. (2000). "Internet Domain Survey, July 2000." www.isc.org/ds/WWW-200007/index.html.

internet.com Corp. (1999). "Half of U.S. College Students Prepared to Surf Internet." http://cyberatlas.internet.com/big_picture/demographics/article /0,1323,5901_158251,00.html.

internet.com Corp. (2000). "Demographics of the Net Getting Older." http://cyber atlas.internet.com/big_picture/demographics/article/0,,5901_448131,00.html.

internet.com Corp. (2001). "Residential High-Speed Access Takes Big Step in 2000." http://cyberatlas.internet.com/markets/broadband/article /0,,10099_583711,00.html.

Karon, R. (2000, January–March). "Bankers Go Online." *E-Learning, 1,* 38–40.

Kestenbaum, T. (1998). "Educational Benefits of Online Learning." http://support.blackboard.net/components/Benefits_of_Online_Learning.doc.

Kroll, L. (1999, March 8). "Good Morning, HAL." *Forbes Magazine.* http://www.forbes.com/global/1999/0308/0205032a.html.

Lieb, J. (2000). "1999 U.S./Canada Internet Demographic Study." www.commerce.net/research/stats/analysis/99-USCanda-Study.pdf.

Mack, J. (1999). "A Net Record: 1 Billion Page Views per Day." www.zdnet.com/eweek/stories/general/0,11011,2398564,00.html.

Maher, K. (1998, August). "Inventing the Virtual Classroom." *Interactivity Magazine, 4.*

McGee, M.K. (1998, June 22). "Save On Training." *InformationWeek.* http://www.informationweek.com/688/88iutra.htm.

Moe, M. (1999). *The Book of Knowledge: Investing in the Growing Education and Training Industry.* New York: Merrill Lynch.

Monahan, T. (1998). "Disseminating Time- and Regulation-Sensitive Information: Online Training Seminars at Mortgage Bankers Association of America." *Distance Training.* San Francisco: Jossey-Bass.

National Telecommunications and Information Administration. (2000). *Falling Through the Net: Toward Digital Inclusion.* Washington, DC: U.S. Department of Commerce. http://www.ntia.doc.gov/ntiahome/digitaldivide/execsumfttn00 .htm.

Nua Inc. (2000a). "How Many Online?" www.nua.ie/surveys/how_many_online/index.html.

Nua Inc. (2000b). "NielsenNetRatings: U.S. Home Internet Access Climbs to 56 Percent." www.nua.ie/surveys/?f=VS&art_id=905356265&rel=true.

Nua Inc. (2000c). "Global Internet Audience Passes 400m Mark." www.nua.ie /surveys/index.cgi?f=VS&art_id=905356267&rel=true.

Picard, D. (1996, November). "The Future Is Distance Training." *TRAINING, 33*(11), S3–S10. http://www.trainingsupersite.com/archive/.

Porter, P. (1999). "Boeing's Big Experiment." www.ittrain.com/archive/MarchLO_99_8.html.

Rickert, A., and A. Sacharow. (2000). "It's a Woman's World Wide Web." us.media metrix.com/data/MMXI-JUP-WWWW.pdf.

Rickert, A. (2000). *The Dollar Divide: Demographic Segmentation and Web Usage Patterns by Household Income.* New York: Media Metrix.

Riley, R., F. Holleman, and L. Roberts. (2000). *E-Learning: Putting a World-Class Education at the Fingertips of All Children.* Washington: U.S. Department of Education.

Russell, T.L. (1999). "The No Significant Difference Phenomenon." http://teleedu cation.nb.ca/nosignificantdifference/.

Schaaf, D. (1998, September). "What Workers Really Think About Training." *TRAINING, 35*(9), 59–66.

Schutte, J.G. (1997). *Virtual Teaching in Higher Education: The New Intellectual Superhighway or Just Another Traffic Jam?* Northridge, CA: California State University.

Smith, B. (2000). "Training Professionals Believe Technology-Based Learning Will Become the Norm Within Five Years." www.fwhrma.org/may_nl/dbm.htm.

Strategis Group. (2000). "U.S. Households with Internet Access to Nearly Double to 90 Million by 2004." www.strategisgroup.com/press/pubs/intdbl.html.

Telcordia Technologies. "Internet Sizer." (2000). www.netsizer.com.

Terry, L. (1998). "Slash Your Costs! Here Comes Web-Based Training." www.solu tionsintegrator.com.

United Nations. (2001). "Cyberschoolbus: Country at a Glance." www.un.org/pubs/CyberSchoolBus/.

University of Phoenix. (2000). "University of Phoenix Online." www.uofphx.quin street.com/html/index.jsp.

Urdan, T.A., and C.C. Weggen. (2000). *Corporate E-Learning: Exploring a New Frontier.* San Francisco: W.R. Hambrecht + Company.

WebSurveyResearch. (2000). "Update on Physicians and the Internet." http://web surveymd.mt01.com/Update_Physicians_Internet.shtml.

Whalen, T., and D. Wright. (2000). *The Business Case for Web-Based Training.* Boston: Artech House.

About the Author

William Horton has been designing technology-based training since 1971 when, as an undergraduate, he designed a network-based course for the Massachusetts Institute of Technology's Center for Advanced Engineering Study. William Horton created www.DesigningWBT.com, wrote e-learning courses on electronic media, designed a network-based knowledge-management system, and served as a member of ASTD's commission on e-learning certification.

William Horton is an internationally sought-after speaker. He recently delivered the keynote addresses for the Human Resources Association National Congress in São Paulo, the Information Technology Training Association conference in Barcelona, and the Knowledge Management Seminarium in Stockholm.

William Horton is a registered Professional Engineer, an MIT graduate, and fellow of the Society for Technical Communication.

William Horton is a prolific author. His books include *Designing Web-Based Training, Designing and Writing Online Documentation,* and *Secrets of User-Seductive Documents.* He is co-author of *Getting Started in Online Learning* and *The Web Page Design Cookbook* and CD-ROM. He is also the author of two more books to be published by ASTD on e-learning: one on evaluating e-learning projects and the other on targeting e-learning precisely.

William and his wife, Kit, the other half of William Horton Consulting, live in downtown Boulder, Colorado, just five blocks east of the Rocky Mountains, in a 100-year old house, which they are lovingly restoring. The kitchen, which he and Kit redesigned themselves, was featured in the April 1999 and September 2000 issues of *Better Homes and Gardens.* You can reach him at william@horton.com.

The Value of Belonging

ASTD membership keeps you up to date on the latest developments in your field, and provides top-quality, *practical* information to help you stay ahead of trends, polish your skills, measure your progress, demonstrate your effectiveness, and advance your career.

We give you what you need most from the entire scope of workplace learning and performance:

Information
We're your best resource for research, best practices, and background support materials – the data you need for your projects to excel.

Networking
We're the facilitator who puts you in touch with colleagues,experts, field specialists, and industry leaders – the people you need to know to succeed.

Technology
We're the clearinghouse for new technologies in training, learning, and knowledge management in the workplace – the background you need to stay ahead.

Analysis
We look at cutting-edge practices and programs and give you a balanced view of the latest tools and techniques – the understanding you need on what works and what doesn't.

Competitive Edge
ASTD is your leading resource on the issues and topics that are important to you. That's the value of belonging!

For more information, or to become a member, please call 1.800.628.2783 (U.S.) or +1.703.683.8100; visit our Website at **www.astd.org**; or send an email to customercare@astd.org.

ASTD

*Linking People,
Learning & Performance*